"FOREIGN COUNTRIES"

CARL H. CLAUDY

CARL H. CLAUDY'S

"Foreign

Countries"

A Gateway to the Interpretation

and Development of Certain Symbols

of Freemasonry

MACOY PUBLISHING & MASONIC SUPPLY CO., INC.
Richmond, Virginia

Printed in the United States of America

To Andrew L. Randell
Himself a Symbol of All That Is Best in
Freemasonry

**THIS LITTLE BOOK OF SYMBOLISM
IS AFFECTIONATELY INSCRIBED**

SONNET

Seers seek for wisdom's flowers in the mind,
  And write of symbols many a learned tome.
      (Grow roses still, though rooted in black loam);
The mystic searches earth till eyes go blind
For soul of roses, yet what use to find
  A spirit penned within a catacomb?
  Nay, all they learn is weightless as sea-foam
That drifts from wave to wave upon the wind.
  In rushes Cap and Bells. How very droll
      The ways of students and the foolish books!
      He finds the secrets of Freemasons' art
In mind nor rose nor tomb nor musty scroll.
  Where no wit is, where all loves are, he looks
      And reads their hidden meaning in his heart.

PUBLISHER'S FOREWORD

CARL H. CLAUDY left a rich legacy to his Masonic brethren with his writings on the Craft which was so dear to his heart. Among such writings, *"Foreign Countries"*, must be classed as one of his finest. It is directed primarily to the Freemason who is just beginning his labors in the Craft, but, we dare say, that both young and old will find new meanings and gain a better vision and understanding of the various ceremonies and symbols of Freemasonry after reading Brother Claudy's interpretations.

To one who has wandered in the lands of symbolism and wished for a guide, to the new Freemason who found little meaning, if any, at the time he was a part of the ceremonies, this book will open vistas never dreamed of and, it is hoped, will give inspiration for a new way of life.

We suggest that one read the last chapter first and then read it again when he comes to the end of the book. He will then understand why the author chose the fitting title *"Foreign Countries"* for this book.

THE PUBLISHERS

Richmond, Virginia
1971

PREFACE

ALBERT PIKE, greatest of Masons as he was greatest of mystics, says, *"Masonry . . . follows the ancient manner of teaching. Her symbols are the instructions she gives; and the lectures are but often partial and insufficient one-sided endeavors to interpret those symbols. He who would become an accomplished Mason must not be content merely to hear or even to understand the lectures, but must, aided by them, and they having as it were marked out the way for him,* STUDY, INTERPRET AND DEVELOP THE SYMBOLS FOR HIMSELF."

This little book is but the interpretation and the development of certain symbols, as one Master Mason has studied them for himself. It is doubtful if the deep student here finds anything new, unless, indeed, the method of presentation may be to him, novel.

The writer has, naturally, what pride and satisfaction may come to any Master Mason who has sought a "covered" meaning and found it, in his heart; apart from that, he offers these little essays on a few of the symbols of Ancient Craft Masonry, knowing that they are very humble attempts at gleaning in the fields whence many a great teacher has reaped. If to any Freemason who reads them comes even a small modicum of Masonic nourishment, then the long day of their writing will be well ended, and the author content that he has helped some brother to "look to the East."

CARL H. CLAUDY.

WASHINGTON, D. C.
November, 1925.

CONTENTS

ENTERED

1– *Language of the Heart*

FREEMASONRY teaches by symbols. Why? Why does she veil in allegory and conceal in object or picture a meaning quite different from its name? Why should Freemasonry express immortality with acacia, brotherly love with a trowel, the world by a lodge, and right-living by a Mason's tools?

That Freemasonry conceals in symbols in order to arouse curiosity to know their meaning is often considered the only explanation. But there are many more lofty ideas of why this great system of truth, philosophy and ethics is hidden in symbols.

It is hardly a matter of argument that man has a triple nature; he has a body, and senses which bring him into contact with, and translate the meanings of, the physical world, of earth, air, fire and water, which is about him. He has a brain and a mind, by which he reasons and understands about the matters physical with which he is surrounded. And he has a Something Beyond; call it Soul, or Heart, or Spirit, or Imagination, as you will; it is something which is allied to, rather than a part of, reason, and connected with the physical side of life only through its sensory contacts.

This soul, or spirit, comprehends a language which the brain does not understand. The keenest of minds have striven without success to make this mystic language plain to reason. When you hear music which brings tears to your eyes and grief or joy to your heart, you respond to a language your brain does not understand and cannot explain. It is not with your brain that you love your mother, your child or your wife; it is with the Something Beyond; and the language with which that love is spoken is not the language of the tongue.

A symbol is a word in that language. Translate that symbol into words which appeal only to the mind, and the spirit of the meaning is lost. Words appeal to the mind; meanings not expressed in words appeal to the spirit.

All that there is in Freemasonry, which can be set down in words on a page, leaves out completely the Spirit of the

Order. If we depended on words or ideas alone, the fraternity would not make a universal appeal to all men, since no man has it given to him to appeal to the minds of all other men. But Freemasonry expresses truths which are universal; it expresses them in a universal language, universally understood by all men without words. That language is the language of the symbol, and the symbol is universally understood because it is the means of communication between spirits, souls, hearts.

When we say of Masonry that it is universal we mean the word literally; it is of the universe, not merely of the world. If it were possible for an inhabitant of Mars to make and use a telescope which would enable him to see plainly a square mile of the surface of the earth, and if we knew it and desired, by drawing upon that square mile a symbol, to communicate with the inhabitants of Mars, we would choose, undoubtedly, one with as many meanings as possible; one which had a material, a mental and a spiritual meaning. Such a symbol might be the triangle, the square or the circle. Our supposed Martian might respond with a complementary symbol; if we showed him a triangle, he might reply with the 47th Problem. If we showed him a circle, he might set down 3.141659–the number by which a diameter multiplied becomes a circumference. We could find a language in symbols with which to begin communication, even with all the universe!

Naturally, then, Freemasonry employs symbols for heart to speak to heart. Imagination is heart's collection of senses. So we must appeal to the imagination when speaking a truth which is neither mental nor physical, and the symbol is the means by which one imagination speaks to another. Nothing else will do; no words can be as effective (unless they are themselves symbols); no teachings expressed in language can be as easily learned by the heart as those which come *via* the symbol through the imagination.

Take from Freemasonry its symbols and you have but the husk; the kernel is gone. He who hears but the words of Freemasonry misses their meaning entirely. Most symbols have many interpretations. These do not contradict but amplify each other. Thus, the square is a symbol of perfection, of rectitude of conduct, of honor and honesty, of good work. These are all different, and yet allied. The square is not a symbol of wrong, or evil, or meanness or disease! Ten different men may read ten different meanings into a square, and yet each meaning fits with, and belongs to the other meanings.

Ten men have ten different kinds of hearts. Not all have the same power of imagination. They do not all have the same ability to comprehend. So each gets from a symbol what he can. He uses his imagination. He translates to his soul as much of the truth as he is able to make a part of him. This the ten cannot do with truths expressed in words. "Twice two is equal to four" is a truth which must be accepted all at once, as a complete exposition, or not at all. He who can understand but the "twice" or the "equal" or the "four" has no conception of what is being said. But ten men can read ten progressive, different, correct and beautiful meanings into a trowel, and each be right as far as he goes. The man who sees it merely as an instrument which helps to bind has a part of its meaning. He who finds it a link with operative Masons has another part. The man who sees it as a symbol of man's relationship to Deity, because with it he (spiritually) does the Master's work, has another meaning. All these meanings are right; when *all* men know all the meanings, the need for Freemasonry will have passed away.

We use symbols because only by them can we speak the language of the spirit, each to each, and because they form an elastic language, which each man reads for himself according to his ability. Symbols form the only language which is thus elastic, and the only one by which spirit can be touched. To suggest that Freemasonry use any other would be as revolutionary as to remove her Altars, meet in the public square or elect by a majority vote. Freemasonry without symbols would not be Freemasonry; it would be but dogmatic and not very erudite philosophy, of which the world is full as it is, and none of which ever satisfies the heart.

2 – Before Knocking

THE man who would be a Freemason comes at once in contact with what may be called the mechanics of the fraternity. These, constantly in view from the very beginning, guide his footsteps through the paths of initiation, and mould his conduct as a Master Mason. He is fortunate, indeed, whose vision enables him to see beyond the flying wheels and levers and catch a vision of the motive power behind. All too many accept the mechanism as the motive power; find in the machinery both a beginning and an end, and so never become Freemasons in the inner meaning of the word.

Why should a word have an inner meaning? Why should a degree have mechanics and an explained meaning, and then, further off and more difficult to see, a concealed meaning, "covered" is the Masonic term, which must be searched for? That is a question which faces every seeker after Masonic light, not even waiting to confound him as he becomes of the Order, but touching him with its mystery as soon as he applies for the degrees!

Freemasonry begins teaching the profane long before they apply for membership. Her reputation is her first contact with the un-elect; she is secret; she is universal; she has enlisted the interest and the services of great and good men for hundreds of years; she is devoted to education, to charity and to good works, and boasts never of any of these; she is reserved and dignified and makes no public parade; she never seeks. These things all intelligent people know. What they do not know is that there are hidden reasons for all these, which thus become symbols "covering" meanings which none but Freemasons ever fully understand, and which some who wear the pin and pay the dues never do comprehend.

Many men desire to become Freemasons without any intelligent appreciation of what they ask. To a great many, Freemasonry is "just a secret society, good fellows; I'd like to belong." Careless talk by coarse-grained men of Masonic "goats" and initiation "tortures" have soiled the idea of

Freemasonry in many minds. But even the unthinking are brought to a sudden pause when they meet the question "Do you believe in God?" Men would hardly start thus to play with goats!

There is more to the question than meets the eye. It is a symbol, as well as a question; among the first with which Freemasonry greets her would-be candidates.

It may be doubted if there ever was a man who didn't believe in God; certainly the self-confessed atheist is as easily silenced and as puerile in his arguments as he is rare. Yet Freemasonry, which demands the simple confession of faith, asks no questions as to what God, nor even what kind of a God. The candidate-to-be may name Him by any syllables; Freemasonry cares not. That she does not care is one of her dearest symbols, since by this very lack she teaches to all her sons that brotherhood is not in a Name, but in hearts; that men may believe in God, Jehovah or Great First Cause; in Love, Confucius, Mithra or a Cosmic Urge, and still be children of one Father, and therefore brethren in the true meaning of the word.

The man who asks his friend to take his petition into his lodge touches his second Masonic symbol. Only by the good offices of a *friend* may he ask for the privileges of Freemasonry. Freemasonry differs, then, from the school, the college, the job, the business house, the life-assurance society; to these the stranger may apply, as indeed, he may apply to many organizations. To Freemasonry he may make no application without the good offices of a friend. When his application is acted upon, a committee is appointed, charged with the duty of ascertaining what manner of man he is, whether he is of sound mind, sound body, freeborn, under the tongue of good report, a reputable citizen, able to support himself and family, and, in the words of the Old Charges, no "stupid atheist or irreligious libertine."

It is obvious that a man is not accepted at his face value by Freemasonry. If Freemasonry does not accept a man from his general appearance, or even from his general reputation, it must be because she knows that a man is not always what he appears to be. In the opinion of the fraternity man has both an inner and an outer aspect; he may be freeborn and sound in mind and limb; he may be "under the tongue of good report" so far as the friend who recommends him knows, but the fraternity insists upon further knowledge; it is the inner man for which she searches; it is the spiritual man she would understand, before she confers the benefits of her rites, her secrets, and her brotherhood.

Emphasis is placed on this preliminary symbol, this investigation, this searching, because it holds the keynote to all of Freemasonry's methods of teaching. It appears a very obvious course to pursue, and ninety-nine out of a hundred accept it as such. "Of course they want to know what sort of a man I am!" argues the prospective candidate. "They don't want to associate with bad men. They don't want to accept an object of charity. They want regular fellows; well, let 'em investigate!" But the hundredth man pauses to wonder how Freemasonry came to know so well that there is an outward and physical and an inward and spiritual man, and that it is the inward and spiritual only which must count in Freemasonry!

We who are old in the Craft know too well that the ideal is often toppled in the dust by the careless committee; that men quite otherwise than "good and true" get into the fraternity. Perhaps more get in than we know; if so, then some of them are lifted up by what they find. We may never learn their true character if they change it after they are subjects of Freemasonry's gentle art! Perhaps it is the will of the Great Architect that we work always with some imperfect material to prove what manner of builders we are! But the fact that men less than good do become Freemasons, at times, has nothing to do with Freemasonry's teaching, long before the door is reached, that man must not be judged by exterior alone, that even a friend may be mistaken about him, and that only a careful digging in the depths will reveal what he really is "in his heart."

3 - Swaddling Clothes

THE Entered Apprentice passes through the period of early Masonic youth. The Fellowcraft is emblematic of manhood; while the Master Mason learns that true Freemasonry gives to a man a well-spent life, and assurance of a glorious immortality.

When newly born into the world, a human baby is the most helpless of all animals. His first tender years are wholly a time of learning; learning to eat, learning to manage his arms and legs, learning to walk, learning to make himself understood, learning to understand. The period an Entered Apprentice must spend before he can receive the degree of Fellowcraft corresponds to these early years of childhood; he must learn to manage his Masonic limbs, must learn to understand Masonic language, and to make himself understood in it.

The Entered Apprentice is more like a child in an institution than like one in a home. In the home the child has the undivided attention of his parents; in the institution he has, necessarily, only the divided attention of those who must mother and father many children, and the help he individually receives is less as the number who claim it is greater. The lodge is an institution; the Entered Apprentice receives careful instruction in the necessary arts of Masonry, in so far as he is prepared to receive them, but, obviously, there can be no coddling, no tender individual attentions which are not also given to all other Entered Apprentices of the lodge.

One child stands out above another in its development in an institution because of its inherent brightness, and because of its willingness to study and to learn. The Entered Apprentice Mason stands out above his fellows as he pays strict attention to those brethren who are his instructors, and as he is willing to study and to learn. For monitors, no matter how great their erudition, and how large their charity and willingness to serve, can only point the path, and give those elementary instructions in Freemasonry which are the *minimum* with which a man can walk onward.

The feet of the initiate have been set upon a path. In his hands has been thrust the staff of ritual, the bread of knowledge, and the water of prayer. With these alone he can proceed up the path to the wall marked "Fellowcraft," and the strait gate through which he can pass only if he has digested the bread, drunk the water and still has the staff. But one climbs the quicker, sees more of the beauties by the way, and arrives with greater strength for the next highway, if not content with the *least* aids, but demands a greater equipment.

The Monitor is a small book which contains all of the ritual of the three degrees, which may be printed. A careful study of it will recall much of the Entered Apprentice Degree, and suggest many questions; questions which any thinking candidate must ask, and queries which, answered, will make him a better Entered Apprentice. The answers to many of these questions are in many good books on Freemasonry. Any Entered Apprentice who will read and ponder a good volume which deals with the first degree of Freemasonry (even so humble a one as this!), will approach the West Gate for his Fellowcraft Degree in a more humble attitude, a more reverent spirit, and with a happier and more confident heart than he who is satisfied merely with his staff, his bread, and his water.

For Freemasonry is old, old. No man knoweth just how old, but deep students of the art have gathered unimpeachable evidence; evidence of the character which would be convincing in a court of law, that the principles which underlie Freemasonry and which are taught in her symbolism, go back beyond the dawn of written history. Freemasonry's symbols are found wherever the physical evidences of ancient civilizations are unearthed. Secret orders of all ages, all climes, all peoples, have, independently of each other, sought the Great Truths along the same paths, and concealed what they found in much the same symbols. Freemasonry is the repository of the learning of the ages, a storehouse of the truths of life and death, religion, and immortality; aye, even of the truths we know regarding the Great Architect of the Universe, which have been painfully won, word by word and line by line, from the books of nature and of the inquiring mind, by literally thousands of generations of men.

No man has a mind big enough, quick enough, open enough, to absorb and understand in an evening even the introduction to what Freemasonry knows; not in a month of evenings! No degree, no matter how impressively performed, can possibly take him far along this road. All that the Entered Apprentice Degree can do is to point the way, and give the seeker sustenance by which he may travel.

One may travel with ears closed, and eyes upon the ground. One will arrive, physically, even as a traveler with bandaged eyes may arrive after a toilsome journey. But to travel thus is not to learn. And the Freemason who does not learn, what sort of a Freemason is he? Pin wearer, only: denying himself of the opportunity to make himself truly one of the greatest brotherhood the world has ever known.

Therefore, use the month or more which is given between the Entered Apprentice and the Fellowcraft Degree, not only to receive monitorial instruction and learn, letter perfect, the ritual in which so much more is hidden than is revealed, but also to investigate, to read, to learn the meaning of some of Freemasonry's symbols and how they came to be.

There are lodge members who will say that all of Freemasonry which any man needs to know is found in the degrees. So are there those who say that all any man needs to know of God or religion is found in the Great Light which rests upon our holy Altar. But be not discouraged by these, nor put faith in the vision of any guide; the only eyes with which any man may truly see are his own; the only faith which is truly valuable to any man is his own. Every man needs an educator in Holy Writ to expound for him the hidden truths which are in the Great Light. Every initiate requires some writer or student to expound for him the hidden truths which are in Freemasonry's ritual and symbols. A legion of devoted men of God have spent thousands of years digging in the

Book of Books, and always have they discovered some new treasure. Generations of men have sought in the mountain which is Freemasonry for the gold which is Truth of God, and found it; without such patient delving, the gold could not be seen. Each should dig for himself, but dig by the light of the lamps lit by those who have gone this way before.

This United States of ours has its ritual; its Declaration of Independence, its Constitution, its Bill of Rights. Doubtless the reader has read all of these; perhaps, in school, he memorized them, as the initiate must memorize Masonic ritual. But the mere learning by heart of the Declaration of Independence or the Constitution never made any man an authority upon them.

The foreigner investigating our institutions for the first time could hardly become a good American merely by such memorization. The highest tribunal in all the world, the Supreme Court, has to interpret to us our own Constitution, and not yet have any legislators come to the end of the meanings of those liberties for which we declared when this country first lifted up its head among the nations of the world, and cried the birth cry.

An Entered Apprentice is barely born, Masonically. He must learn, and learn well, if he is to enter into his heritage. That which is worth having is worth working for. Experience in life teaches that what comes without labor turns soon to ashes in the mouth. Without labor there can be no rest; without work there can be no vacation; without pain there can be no pleasure; without sorrow there is no joy. And equally true it is that, while men do receive the degrees of Freemasonry at the hands of their brethren, there is no Freemasonry in a man's heart if he is not willing to sacrifice some time, give some effort, some study, ask some questions, digest some philosophy, to make it truly his own.

An initiate is called an "Entered Apprentice" when there has been performed over him and with him a certain ceremony, but no man can in reality be "entered" *unless he is willing to enter.* There is homely truth in many an old saying. The horse who is led to the water will not drink if he is not thirsty; no man can make him swallow if he will not. Freemasonry, in conferring the distinction of the Entered Apprentice Degree, brings her initiate through a green pasture, to lie down beside the still water of her truth. But there lives not the Grand Master of any jurisdiction, all powerful in Freemasonry though he is, who can make him drink of those waters; there lives not the man, be he king, prince or potentate, with no matter what temporal power or what strength of army or of wealth, who can force him through the door his brethren have swung wide.

To all initiates, then, let it be said: The pathway is before you. The staff, the bread, the water are in your hand. Whether you will travel blindly and in want, or eagerly and with joy, depends only and wholly upon you.

And very largely upon what you now do, how soon you emerge from your swaddling clothes, and how well you learn, will depend the epitaph some day to be written of your memory on the hearts of your fellow lodge members; it is for you to decide whether they will say of you: " Just another lodge member," or "A true Freemason, a faithful Son of Light."

4 – Blind

WHERE we see plainly, there is no mystery. The Freemason learns to differentiate between a "secret" and a "mystery." A "secret" is something known to those who keep it, something which may be told to the privileged, something to be kept from those who may not know it. A "mystery," in the Masonic sense, is that which is concealed but which may be discovered; that which is concealed not by laws or promises, but hidden only from its very nature. In Freemasonry it is not a "secret" that a candidate must express his belief in Deity. But Deity is and must always be a "mystery" to us all, even though we penetrate a little way into its glory through the gentle administrations of Freemasonry .

A candidate is temporarily deprived of his vision on entering a Masonic lodge, not because there is anything there he must not see, or anything to be seen which is not, later, shown to him, but as a symbol that he is mentally blind; that he is in a state of darkness, and that only through the ministrations and by the consent of his brethren, is he to be "brought to light."

The candidate naturally puts his own interpretations upon a Masonic degree. The manner of his preparation for entrance to a lodge room may appeal to him as "unnecessary," perhaps as "funny." But unless he be a moron, he can hardly fail to appreciate the significance of his preparation when he has become an Entered Apprentice. Nor can he find humor in a reverent approach to the Altar on which lies the Holy Bible. The preparation is thus a "mystery"; to win to a true understanding of its symbolism one must understand that Freemasonry is a birth, a bringing into existence of a new ideal in a man's heart.

Man is born without raiment; he is born helpless; he is born dependent upon those who love him for everything that makes life possible. The candidate for the Entered Apprentice Degree must be born again, before he is really *entered*; and when his preparation is so regarded, the rite becomes solemn, convincing, sacred; there is no humor in it, nor any intention or desire to wound the most sensitive feelings. The initiate does but go the same way as all good brothers who have preceded him through the West Gate. As they traveled, so must he; as they received the Masonic rebirth, so must he; as they proved themselves worthy of it, so must he, if Freemasonry is to be to him what it can be, if he will let it; such an ennobling influence in life as can be given by no other fraternal organization on the face of the earth.

To be blindfolded, then, or "hoodwinked," to use the Masonic term, is not to be deprived of sight that one be unresisting to what is to be done; it is not a removal of defenses against the brethren, but is symbolic of a state of darkness, blindness, a lack of knowledge.

As he progresses further in the art of Freemasonry, the thoughtful candidate discovers that the three degrees as a whole are symbols of human life. The Entered Apprentice Degree, of course, is a symbol of birth, infancy and childhood. The Fellowcraft Degree is a symbol of young but complete manhood and the struggle of life. The Master Mason Degree is symbolical of age, a well-spent life, knowledge, and the reward; a happy and contented age with the hope of a glorious immortality just beyond.

Some animals are born blind. The human baby "sees" only in the sense that light creates a sensation in the eyes; he must learn to focus his eyes, to distinguish shapes and colors. Men born blind who have later had sight restored have had to "learn to see" just as men weakened by illness have to learn to walk. As an Entered Apprentice, a candidate is blind to all that Freemasonry teaches; blind to her secrets and her mysteries, her philosophy and her doctrine, her beliefs and her certain knowledge. There is, then, the best of reasons for hoodwinking the candidate, that he may have impressed upon him his state of darkness, and place him in an humble frame of mind that he may receive the light in reverence and in gratitude.

No thinking man believes that Freemasonry has created a special brand of knowledge, denied to the profane, with which she blesses those who partake of her brotherhood. Freemasonry has not created any knowledge. Man does not create knowledge. He discovers facts, draws conclusions from those facts, tests the conclusions in practice, finds them true, and calls them knowledge. There have always been radio waves; only recently have we taken them into our minds as "knowledge." There has always been God; compared to the age of man on earth, it is only recently that we have come to any knowledge of Him. There has always been the principle of brotherhood; there has always been the philosophy and the truth which Freemasonry teaches; but only since Freemasonry gathered together and made her own the scattered knowledge, from here, from there, which the peoples of the world in their many rites, secret societies, mysteries and orders had collected, have these principles been available for teaching in one fraternal body, by one group of men, to those fit to receive them.

Freemasonry has no "secrets" of value to the world. Her "secrets" are valuable only to her brethren. But her "mysteries," her teachings, her philosophy, are all of great value to the world, and none so anxious as Freemasonry to give them forth freely to all men who can assimilate them. But much of the world is in spiritual darkness; much of the world is yet "hoodwinked" by passion, by prejudice, by ignorance, by malice and envy and self-seeking. Not until those hoodwinks are removed by the Master Brother, Experience, can those so blinded see the Masonic light, or have the permission of those who walk in its radiance to partake with them of its effulgence.

The preparation, then, which the candidate undergoes is wholly symbolic; he who *understands* the solemn experience of being brought for the first time to light in Freemasonry will value more and appreciate to a greater degree that which has been done to him. It is a matter for prayerful gratitude that brethren, banded together, sharing the same knowledge and travelling the same road, remove from the eyes of the profane the hoodwink of ignorance and replace it with the illumination of knowledge; it is this of which the blinded eyes are a symbol.

As there is no gift within the power of the All Powerful which a blind man would rather have than sight, so to the initiate, no act of initiation should be more gratefully received, or with deeper reverence, than the removal of the hoodwink and the blessed privilege of joining one's brethren in the full and free use of the Masonic Light.

5 – Entry

IN the Entered Apprentice Degree, the initiate is introduced at once to one of the most solemn, most inspiring and most beautiful ceremonies in all Freemasonry; he meets, at the very outset, a symbol which should impress him deeply for all time, that Freemasonry is not of the earth, earthy, but is concerned almost entirely with the spirit.

Alas, too few there are who know at the time the loveliness they encounter. Too anxious, too concerned with what a "degree" may be, too frightened often (more's the pity!), with idle tales of unthinking brethren who seek to impress a would-be initiate with the "terrors" of an initiation, the candidate experiences without understanding, knows without comprehending, feels, without sensing, a moment which in after years will come back to him as a fragrant memory of beauty.

Almost at once, a candidate is reminded of trust in the Great Architect, of the benefits of the prayers of his brethren-to-be, and instructed that in their care there is no danger to be feared.

Simple? Man, it is sublime! This "simple" ceremony; aye, simple, as all beauty is simple, simple as all greatness is simple; is at once the beginning and the end, the Alpha and Omega of Freemasonry. Pass it not over lightly, for it may serve as the beginning for thought which will take years to finish.

Freemasonry's lodges are erected to God. Cathedrals, monuments, shrines, are erected to God. To "erect to God" means literally to raise up toward Him. Symbolically, to "erect to God" means to construct something in honor, in worship, in reverence to and for Him. Hardly is the initiate within the West Gate before he is impressed that Freemasonry worships God . . . God under any name the initiate pleases, of course, since no applicant for the degrees is required to define the God in Whom he believes . . . that Freemasonry is a God-loving organization. Carrying out the symbolism of the building trades, Freemasons refer to the Great Architect of the Universe, surely a reverent and an expressive term.

The initiate receives two solemn assurances from his brethren-to-be. He hears the inspiring words of a petition to Deity; asking what? Asking for something for those who pray? No, asking a blessing upon him who comes thus helpless, defenceless and alone to the lodge at the West Gate of which he has knocked. The prayers differ somewhat in different jurisdictions, but their intent is the same. Here is the one the writer heard:

"Vouchsafe thine aid, Almighty Father of the Universe to this our present convention; and grant that this candidate for Masonry may dedicate and devote his life to Thy service and become a true and faithful brother among us. Endue him with a competency of thy Divine Wisdom, that, by the secrets of our art, he may be better enabled to display the Beauties of Holiness, to the honor of thy holy name. Amen. So mote it be."

And this ceremony is immediately followed by the admonition to the candidate that he follow fearlessly, that there is no danger here! He is in the hands of friends! Helpless, they will help him; blind, they will see for him; ignorant, they will instruct him; tender, they will guard him; in darkness, they will bring him to light.

Among the most beautiful of Freemasonry's symbols, these express at the very beginning the fundamental principle of Freemasonry: the Fatherhood of God, and the Brotherhood of man.

There are many men, and of course there are as many minds as men. It is but natural that a large number fail to appreciate the significance of the first entry into a Masonic lodge, and the all-embracing character of its solemnity. So raising their feet high as they walk lest an unseen wire trip them; men flinch and hang back, lest an unseen obstacle be struck. Shame to the brethren who have created such an impression! Shame to the lodge which permits its initiates to come through the West Gate without such mental and spiritual preparation as will forever remove such an unworthy attitude of mind!

But there are many brethren who will see to it that the candidate does understand; one here labors in this work, humbly and with a contrite heart, to offer the feeble glimmer of his rush light. Freemasonry is among the noblest conceptions of all mankind; Freemasonry's first ceremonies express love of God, love of brother for brother, faith in a power above, faith in the strong arm of fraternal love. Who has eyes to read and willingness to learn; let him not turn this page without taking to his heart the glorious symbolism of this "simple" ceremony of entry, which strikes the chord on which all of Freemasonry's magnificent harmonies are based.

There is much in Freemasonry's degrees which cannot be discussed in print. There are parts of this ceremony of entry into a Masonic lodge which will make a deep impression on the mind, and which can only adequately be explained by the good offices of some brother who may speak, not write, with the willing and informed tongue to the attentive ear. Depend not upon the degree itself wholly for enlightenment; the knowledge received in the degrees is but a tool. Only the possessor may use it. Never the school or the instructor who may teach; all the best of schools, the most learned of "teachers" may do is to set forth the knowledge, the road to more learning.

The experienced Freemason has long ago made it his duty and pleasure to find, in his lodge, that brother who can answer his questions and explain that which may not be printed. He needs no further admonitions. But to the young Freemason, let it be here repeated: "Seek, and ye shall find."

If what has here been set down has reached any candidate's heart with even a modicum of the reverence with which it has been written, he will have for all time a new love for the first ceremonies of Freemasonry, and a new gratitude that it has been his splendid fortune to have a part in them.

6 – East to West, by South

WHAT might be denominated the "casual" seeker after Masonic light is far more apt to be impressed with the mechanics than the meaning of a degree. Men seek Masonry for many reasons; some because of the good repute of the Order; some because friends or relatives are Master Masons; some because of curiosity or a desire to belong to a "secret" society. Many who come to scoff remain to pray. Perhaps those who at first find the outward ceremonies of greater interest than their inner meaning are blameless, but it is certain that a knowledge of the inner meaning gives much real pleasure, as well as instruction.

Hardly is an initiate well within the West Gate than he takes part in the Rite of Circumambulation, one of the oldest rites in all history; older, perhaps, than baptism. The man who is intrigued by the mechanics of the degree will see only men walking about a lodge room; he may even consider it a meaningless ceremony, perhaps arranged to "fill up the time," perhaps to afford opportunity for those readings from the Great Light which accompany it. But he who considers it so misses the inner meaning; even he who finds in the circumambulation an opportunity for the brethren to satisfy themselves that their initiate is properly prepared, goes but a short way along the road of knowledge of what this rite really is.

Could we, by any chance, send back our eyes, as we may send our thoughts, to a far-off time, our organs of vision would travel a long way before they saw the first men who walked about a central point as a means of worship of that which they held Most High.

Long before the earliest written or stone-recorded history of man, worshippers must have traveled around, and again around, in their ceremonies. The earliest known practices of this character were too well developed, too purposeful, to have been the first performances.

Among the very earliest of religions was worship of the sun. What more natural than that a brutish man, just struggling from beastliness to the dawn of abstract thought, should have considered the sun as the All Powerful Deity which all men have always known was somewhere? The sun gave light and heat. The sun protected men from the ravages of wild beasts. When the sun shone, they were comfortable and happy. When their god hid his face behind a cloud and wept, they were cold, uncomfortable. Without the sun, nothing grew; with it, food for man, and food for his food, the beasts, was plentiful. It required no great stretch of imagination for ignorant savages to see in the sun the very body of God Himself.

What was next to God? If rain was His tears, if lightning His anger and thunder His voice, if the wind was His arm and the earthquake His revenge, was not fire His very self? Fire kept away beasts; as did the sun. Fire warmed and comforted, as did the sun. Fire punished and burned, as did the sun.

Man must early have acquired fire; fire was all about him, in the volcano, the hot spring, the lightning flash, the grass fire set from hot sun through a dewdrop lens. Some say fire worship preceded sun worship, but here it makes no difference which. Worship of sun in the sky meant worship of fire upon the rude altar of stones, no matter which religion is the older.

As man is incurably religious, so is he incurably imitative. He imitates that which he admires. The small boy wants to be like father and struts with a cane and wears Daddy's hat. Small sister trails her mother's skirt upon the ground and wears a ring like mother while playing at keeping house and mothering dolls. The humble soldier imitates his general. The clerk imitates his executive. The poor man apes the rich. The ideal of Christianity is that men imitate and try to be like the Christn.

Savage man, too, had his admirations, and his imitations. The sun he could imitate, in heat, only by building a fire, which to some extent he could control. But the sun moved; the sun arose each morning in one part of the heavens, travelled slowly and majestically and unhurriedly across, through another part of the heavens, to go to rest again in still another part of the heavens.

In our language, the sun rises in the east, mounts to the zenith and passes to its setting in the west by way of the south.

Early caveman walked from his "east," travelled to the west by way of the south, and returned again by way of the north, then with them, as now with us, a place of darkness.

Such must have been the origin of the rite of circumambulation; an imitation, by its worshippers, of that sun which was their God. Those long dead, altogether forgotten, prehistoric ancestors of ours, walking in awed procession about their bit of fire on a stone, laid the foundation of that rite of circumambulation which every secret society, every mystery, every religion in all times, has made a part of itself.

Today, as Free and Accepted Masons, travelling about our holy Altar on which is the fire of the word of God, we still walk from the east to the west, by way of the south. Only once in the three degrees, as all Master Masons know, is the direction reversed. At that time the travel by way of the north means to us just what it meant to our long dead ancestors: death.

Thus, this rite of circumambulation has the respectability of antiquity, and means far, far more than it appears; it is not done to "give time" for a passage from Scripture nor to "take time" because there is nothing else to do. It is a reminder to Freemasons that God can best be worshipped by humble imitation of those virtues He has let us see are Godlike; that as Freemasons we walk always in the light of His word, and the shadow of His presence, and that Freemasonry, instead of being, as the historian of written fact insists she must be, but a few hundred years old, reaches across the crushing years afar off, and makes her own the earliest wisdom of the first men who picked one of His marvels to be their Deity.

7 – World

WHAT is a lodge? Why is a lodge a lodge, and not a chapter or a councilor a club, or some other name? Why is a lodge an "oblong square" and what, if any, is the meaning of this contradictory term?

All these are perfectly reasonable questions which any initiate may expect to have answered; but his expectation is not met, unless he inquires; the ritual is silent about these matters.

"Lodge" is a good old English word, meaning to house, to shelter, and thus, a house or shelter; today the "porter's lodge" is in fact a house or cottage, but its name is "lodge."

Our operative brethren, from whom we sprang, must necessarily have had a place in which they found lodging. Workmen, craftsmen, Masters, gathered from afar off to build a great Cathedral. Their homes were elsewhere. They had to have food and shelter. So they built a house for themselves; it was their "lodge" and of course their meeting place. What more natural than that their word should have come to mean also their organization, as it means ours?

But there is an even older meaning to this symbolism. Man imitates; when he reveres, he imitates the more. Our very ancient progenitors thought of the world as a flat plain; even as recently as the times in which our Great Light was written, there were "the four Corners of the earth," and he was a bold mariner indeed who set sail for and discovered the New World; bold, because all but a few confidently expected he would "sail off the edge" of the world into . . . what?

The world was flat. It had corners. It had a sky. In the sky were stars; lamps. Our ancient brethren, in erecting a house, especially a house to be used for assembly and worship, made it the shape they considered the earth to be. Perhaps because of some dim perception of the beauty to be found in variety, perhaps because there are so many examples of greater length than breadth in nature . . . trees, rivers, many lakes, mountain ranges, valleys . . . it became apart of their belief to conceive of the earth as an "oblong square."

It is only in modern times that a "square" means a rectangle with sides of equal length, each angle of ninety degrees. A rectangle, however, loses nothing of its "squareness" in the sense that the word means ninety degree angles, by having two sides longer than the other two. So while we moderns call one figure a "square," and another an "oblong," when we combine the two words and speak of an "oblong square," we mean the figure which our ancient brethren gave the earth, and, of course, with "square" corners.

This fits in exactly with modern interpretations of our symbols; the Masonic lodge is itself a symbol of the world. By analogy it may also be a symbol of the universe, since "the world" was our ancient brother's all; all he knew of the universe. But it is sufficient if we make it a symbol of the world.

The outer world as we know it is a place of strife, of anxiety, of labor, of dissension, often of bitterness, in which men strive with weapons, sometimes of steel, sometimes of wit and business, against each other. We find much of beauty in the world, but also much of misery; and we see much of that misery caused by dissension, by disagreement, by one man's insistence that he is right and his belief true, while his neighbor is equally intent upon the truth and verity of what he believes to be the reality.

The Masonic lodge, symbol of the world, is also symbol of what Freemasonry believes the world can be. Here are many men, of many minds, of all religions, of all degrees of education, of all professions, of all degrees of wealth and poverty. But the strife which is the world's is not in the Masonic world. Here all kinds of men of all kinds of ideas unite in one universal idea, practice one universal faith, without dogma and without creed. Here they forbear each with the other, and reach hands across their "oblong square" to greet their brother man, solely for what he is in reality, not for what he may have won from the profane world in money, title, power, position, prestige or knowledge.

The lodge is regulated and conducted according to law. It is not a law of coercion, of penalty, or of any one class or man within the lodge. We have our Old Charges, we have the fundamental laws of Freemasonry found in the Ancient Landmarks, and when we disagree among ourselves as to them, we each recognize those of our neighbor under the name of "customs of immemorial antiquity," and obey them just the same! But we also have our Grand Lodge, and its laws. So that the lodge, as a symbol of the world, is still in conformity with the fact. As the world has laws, while acknowledging a Higher Law, so our lodge has its laws, and acknowledges the higher laws of the Grand Lodge.

Here again the lodge sets an example the world is long in following; not for every new crisis, every new evil, every new whim or fancy, is there a new law with a new penalty made in a lodge. The one law of toleration, of forbearance, of brotherly love, has been found to be so all-embracing and so all-potent, that Freemasonry finds no need constantly to make new laws for her lodges; or her lodges, new laws for their members. And it is in the hope, perhaps more felt than expressed, that some far day the whole world will be enabled to live together in comfort and peace and happiness, with only the laws of universal brotherhood, forbearance and toleration, all based on one universal Fatherhood, that Freemasonry keeps her torch alight in the hearts of men. It is in that hope that she casts her illumination, feeble for the eyes which are yet blinded with the Mosaic law idea of "an eye for an eye," glowing and brilliant for those whose spiritual eyes behold not only the "oblong square" but the All Seeing Eye above.

When we conceive of the lodge itself as a symbol of humanity, its government becomes at once an allegory of beauty in law and law in beauty, in which the Master is the servant of his brethren, and the brethren the servants of their Master; in which all are for one, as one will work for all; in which the only punishment, the only coercion, is that moral force of regard for the love of our brethren, that god-like part of man which makes him wish to serve for the love of service.

One said *"inasmuch as ye do it unto the least of these, ye do it also unto me . . ."*

8 – A Voice Thunders

FREEMASONRY has been most unreasonably and unjustly criticised by those who do not understand her, because of two features of her ritual and organization; the use of the Altar, and the administration of obligations to initiates.

There is no law, secular or divine, which reserves for any special organization the use of an altar. From the beginning of Biblical history, men built altars for themselves; it was not necessary that the altars be a part of a church, or a tribe, or a religion. Any man, no matter where he might be, erected his pile of stones, placed thereon the fagots he gathered and made his "burnt offering" to Jehovah. Religion, when organized, swiftly adopted the altar as its own, but, side by side with its practice, ran that of many secret societies, systems of philosophy and mysteries which preserved and transmitted knowledge, keeping a holy fire alight on altars consecrated to a god, or to an idea.

Freemasonry, keeping her holy fire alight on her Altars, robs no church. Nor is she alone in this practice; many another organization possesses a holy place, and, indeed, every man erects an altar in his heart. It may be a hearth fire, a woman's face, a pair of childish arms about his neck; but an altar, a holy place, a focus of pure thought and a home for the inner spirit, must be in every man's life.

The Altar of Freemasonry, then, is much more than a mere excrescence upon the floor, supporting a Book of the Law and the Square and Compasses. During the war one saw lodges with the Altars extended in form, sometimes with boards, sometimes with kitchen tables, yet no man thought them less holy that they were makeshifts. It is not the material nor the form, but the purpose and the thought, which makes Freemasonry's Altars holy. The Altar in the lodge is the well from which flows the river of brotherhood; the mine from which come the priceless jewels of the five points of fellowship.

In ancient days the rude outdoor altars of savage tribes were provided with horns. A fugitive from justice, or a man fleeing from an enemy, was safe from molestation when he could touch one of those horns. From that day to this, the altar has been a sanctuary. Not with us is it a place of refuge for those who seek to escape physical contests, but a haven from surrounding spiritual dangers. To her glory be it said, Freemasonry fails no man who brings a contrite heart before her Altar, and her sanctuary to the distressed of mind and heart is as real and as powerful as that of those ancient stone piles which provided safety for the sore beset.

Upon our Altar lies a Book of the Law. In this country it is the Holy Bible; in other countries the Book of Faith of the religion there followed. The Altar is thus mute testimony to all men that Freemasonry is founded and rests upon a Fatherhood of God.

The wise initiate sees the Altar, not only by the illumination of the three lesser lights or luminaries, grouped in triangular form about it. He sees it also by that inner light which, like the Shekinah of old about the holy Ark of the Covenant, glows about that which is holy because it is holy. The thoughtful initiate sees in Freemasonry's Altar the source of all that "fraternity" which makes Freemasonry such a "cement of brotherly love" between man and man. In his slow parade about it, when kneeling at it, either with his fellow candidates or, once, spiritually naked and absolutely alone, save for God, he should regard it with reverent eyes as a symbol of the best which is within man, the loveliest thoughts which a human being can think, the humble testimony of the human heart to its absolute dependence upon a Supreme Power .

The initiate at the Altar takes upon himself the most solemn and binding pledge known to man. But it is a great mistake to speak of it as "taking the oath."

The Masonic obligation is not so called, and should not be so thought of. The oath is a mere calling upon That Which is Holy to witness the truth and the sincerity of the protestation made. "So help me, God," is the most binding of oaths; no elaboration can make it stronger or more difficult to break.

The Masonic obligations are much, much more than mere oaths. They are the essence of Freemasonry; from them comes all that it is. Without them, Freemasonry is not. One can conceive a body of men so situated that there is no building in which to meet; no light by which to see; no clothing to wear; no benches to rest upon, even no Altar of material substance. Yet, given the right spirit and the knowledge, a man might be made a Master Mason under such circumstances. But in the most beautiful Temple ever built; standing before the most magnificent Altar ever erected; with every working tool of Freemasonry about and every convenience at hand, there could be no degree, no brotherhood, no initiation, no passing, no bringing to light, without the obligations.

As the obligations put knowledge within a man's heart which was not there before, they are symbols of wisdom. As they lay duties upon a man's heart which were not his before, they are symbols of Masonic responsibility. As they give to a man relations with other men he never knew before, they are symbols of mutuality. As they demand from him a compliance and a submission not required of him before, they are symbols of obedience. And as they are uplifting, inspiring, unselfish, sublime, they are symbols of spirituality, of man's yearning for God, and humility before Him.

Many a man walks through the degrees and sees the Altar as a decorated piece of furniture with a book and two tools upon it. The same man hears in the obligation merely an oath of silence and a few phrases of altruistic promise. They are the men who see in the rainbow only a colored band, to whom the ocean is but water and the mountain peak but a pile of earth. On such as these the glory of God in nature and the mysteries of Freemasonry are wasted. The true Freemason looks upon the Altar as the holy place of Freemasonry, as the source of all its wonder; and hears in the obligation not only the words, but the thunder of that Voice at which the most courageous must tremble, the most righteous bow in humility, the most independent be obedient.

To all true initiates the obligations are thus symbols of a glory unseen, of a majestic wisdom unheard.

9 – A Light Measures

THERE is no symbol in all Freemasonry of greater power, more impressive in its dignity and drama, or more simple in conception, than the first bringing to light. Alas, that for too many it is not a symbol; merely a ceremony. Yet is it pregnant with meaning, and, if read aright, can be second only to that other astonishing and beautiful conception, the raising to the Sublime Degree.

"In the beginning God created the heaven and the earth. And the earth was without form, and void; and darkness was upon the face of the deep. And the Spirit of God moved upon the face of the waters. And God said, Let there be light: and there was light."

All Entered Apprentice Masons hear this quotation from the Great Light under unforgettable circumstances. Freemasonry has made the passage peculiarly her own, and in it is found an explanation of our symbolic bringing to light. Let us analyze a little.

"In the beginning," at the time of creation, the earth was formless. In the beginning, as an elected initiate, but yet a profane, the candidate is formless, Masonically. He knows nothing. He is void of Masonic intelligence. In this condition, truly, he is in darkness. Darkness broods for him, "on the face of the deep." It is to be hoped that it is "a deep" over which profane darkness reigns; Freemasonry tries to choose those men whose hearts are deep, not shallow; whose minds are not mere holes in the surface. The initiate is in darkness, yet Freemasonry, trusting to the judgment of the committee and of the brethren and to the "tongue of good report," believes that there is depth here, even if unillumined; believes that the Masonic light may show something therein worth seeing.

"The Spirit of God moved." The Great Intelligence was about to do a mighty thing–to bring light to the world. With us, the brethren are reverently about to do for the initiate that which may have a mighty effect upon his whole life–they are about to bring him to light.

Actually, it is an unblinding of the eyes, that he may see the light, and also the lights, of Freemasonry. Spiritually, it is an unveiling of the mind, that it may partake freely and in confidence of the feast of brotherhood and fraternal knowledge which is about to be spread before him. The initiate who sees in it only a simple ceremony has missed its point, more especially if he is misled about that other part of the ceremony, by which all present assist in this bringing of illumination to the candidate.

No man, no matter how conceited, will agree that he knows more in the aggregate than a great number of men. For all men know something that no other man knows, since no two men upon this earth have exactly the same experience of life. The initiate, then, though he be a professor in a university, must in fairness agree that the many who stand about our Altar to bring him to light have something to teach him. That ceremony in which all take part is at once an offer and a promise. Elsewhere in the ritual the promise is made in words, that he who seeks for light among his brethren will find them as ready to impart what they know of the Mystic Tie as he is ready to receive it. Here the promise is made dramatically, without words. One's brethren . . . brethren now in very truth, since the first obligation has been voluntarily assumed and the confining cable tow has been removed (because Freemasonry now holds the candidate by a far stronger tie than any of material cord) . . . assist in bringing the initiate to light. This is a symbol: what one wishes to know, all are ready to teach; what one wishes to do, all are ready to help in doing; what one hopes to accomplish, all are vitally interested in aiding.

It is intensely symbolic that an initiation into a Masonic lodge is so conducted that upon light being given, the candidate is forced to see, not only light, but the Great Light; not only the illumination of the three lights about the Altar but the great symbolic tools of the Order. For though writers (even as this one!) may elaborate and expound, though lecturers may talk and learned students may dig and delve

into musty tome and ancient record, the whole doctrine of
Freemasonry is contained within the angle of a square, the
points of compasses and the Book of the Law.

Freemasonry brings to the initiate only that which is new
to him. It is not new in reality; it is old, old . . . was old when
Rome fell, old when the pyramids were built; aye, old when
the first caveman sat him down, as did Rodin's "Thinker," to
ponder the mystery about him; old when Lowell's:

". ..*brute despair of trampled centuries*
Leapt up with one hoarse yell and snapt its bands,
Groped for its right with horny callous hands,
And stared around for God with bloodshot eyes."

What Freemasonry brings is not only an old doctrine,
made new for us who are new in the world; she brings us a
yardstick by which we may measure, each of us ourselves,
and, measuring, learn to grow. It is these which we discover
when we are brought to light; the square, by which we measure
that which we build; the compasses, by which we circumscribe
our lives and conduct; the Book of the Law, by which we
keep our feet upon the path marked out for all men.

Says Horace, "Every man should measure himself by his
own standard." There is no foot-rule by which a man may
measure his mind, or his heart. There is no scale by which he
may say of his character, it is so many cubits high and broad,
or so many fathoms deep.

But measurements are not necessarily made in physical
units. The astronomer uses for his yardstick neither feet nor
miles, but the time of the passage of light, and records the
distance of far-off suns in light-years. The physicist can no
more measure the size of a molecule with a scale than he can
weigh a thought with a balance, but he can beat a measured
quantity of gold to a leaf and his pencil will tell him how
sheerly thin it is; he may spread a drop of oil of known size to
its greatest area on water, blow dust on it to mark its edge,
calculate its utter thinness and so arrive at a figure which must

be greater, be it never so small, than the dimension of the molecule.

And a man, if he cannot measure himself with rule or scale, can test himself with those standards which really measure a human soul. If he calls himself Freemason he can set himself beside what his brethren consider a Freemason should be, and see how far short he falls of that stature. If he calls himself a friend, he can look in the glass and see whether his eyes drop when he thinks of how he acts where the object of his friendship is concerned. If he name himself devout Christian or Jew or Mohammedan, he can look to the book of his faith for the measure of his living up to that which he professes.

And if he is content merely to call himself a Man, he can look to those who are acclaimed in history as men in the finest meaning of that term, and see how much within him there is of Washington, who was not afraid, or Father Damien, who looked leprosy in the face and laughed.

Perhaps it is not really so important by what standards we measure, each of us ourselves, as that we do measure. And that is why this bringing to light in Freemasonry is so important as a symbol; it is vitally important that we do measure, by those ancient standards which the Fraternity sets. In the first effulgence of Masonic light the means for measurement are presented. In the first sight of the form of a lodge, all that is Freemasonry in essence is to be seen, even if Masonic light is yet provided but partially. But there is enough light to see by, and enough lesson to live by; there is enough tool to measure by, and enough standard to grow to.

He is a wise initiate, indeed, who searches both his own heart and the hearts of those who have stretched forth their hands to help him into the brightness of Masonic light, for the will to live up to the standard, and the wit to understand that standard by which he, and all Freemasons, will at long last be measured.

10 – Something Beyond

IN every well-regulated lodge there is represented a certain point within a circle. There is, perhaps, no older symbol in all the world than this; almost every religion, every " Ancient Mystery" and many philosophies have used it, found new meanings in it. Freemasonry has taken it for her own, and reads her own meaning into it.

A symbol with so many explanations is obviously one which speaks in different tongues to different men; even to catalog all the meanings which may be taken from it would be wearisome. Within it is contained the germ of all mathematics. It can be interpreted as a symbol of the world, as a symbol of the universe, as a symbol of time and of eternity. As a circle has neither beginning nor end, it is truly symbolical of mystery which is not solvable by human reason; and yet it may, as in the Blue Lodge, be but a symbol of the individual brother and that line beyond which he must not pass if he is to be a true Freemason.

Its origin in Freemasonry, however, is not lost in the mists of antiquity. It seems highly probable that it is a survival of an ancient operative Masonic secret; at least its interpretation in the light of a simple geometrical process makes it beautifully Masonic in the speculative sense.

In the Middle Ages, when the Cathedral builders of Europe were at the height of their glory, education was conspicuous rather by its absence than its presence. Architects and mathematicians there were, otherwise we should have had no great buildings. But the average Fellow of the Craft (who corresponded to what we know as a Master Mason) was a workman with his hands, rather than with his brain. He knew that stones must be square, else his building fell down. He knew that to get them square, he "tried them by the square," for such was taught him by the Masters. But how a square became square was a sealed mystery to most of them.

Tools are either of wood or iron. If squares are made of wood, they warp, become broken, get out of true. If of metal, they can be bent, worn, and so no longer measure a right angle. Therefore it was necessary to *prove* the square frequently. This was one of the Masters' secrets, jealously guarded, and given only to those who had served their apprenticeship and proved their fitness by making a Master's Piece which should pass the inspection of the Masters of the Craft.

Here is a diagram of a circle, with a straight line across it. The line bisects the circle, while passing through the center or "point within a circle." If a single dot be placed *anywhere* on the circumference of the circle (as at "a") and that dot joined by two lines which pass through the points where the straight line cuts the circle (as at "b" and "c"), those two lines will form a right angle.

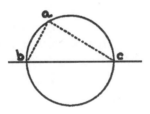

This simple process provides a means by which a square may be tried. Today we use the point within the circle as a measurement for the individual brother, rather than for a working tool; the circle is the boundary beyond which his passions must not lead him. But anciently the circle was the boundary of the right angle. As the Master Mason today may not materially err if he guides himself by the point and the circle, so our ancient brethren guided their squares by the point and the circle and thus kept them from material error.

The earnest student of Masonic light, however, will not be content with this explanation alone; he will see in the circle a symbol of Time, which has neither beginning nor end, and Space, which starts not, neither does it finish. And here the symbol becomes a vast mystery; many men have pondered on the mysteries of time and space, nor yet found an answer which satisfies both mind and heart.

To us, a hundred years is a great span of time, since it is more than we live. Yet in reality the fact that it is more than a man's lifetime doesn't make it long. A week is more than the life of some insects, but a week isn't long. A year may be more than the life of a worm, but that doesn't make it long. A decade may be beyond the span of life of cat or dog–does that make it long?

An Old World fable runs: " At the top of the earth is a rock, a hundred miles long, a hundred miles high, a hundred miles wide. Once every thousand years a little bird comes to the rock to sharpen his beak. When the rock shall have been all worn away by this use, a single day of eternity will have passed by."

What is time? Obviously it isn't a thing; it has no weight, taste, smell, bulk. It has no width, height, depth. Whether it has length, although we measure it in units of length, is open to question. Has a something which possesses none of the qualities which we associate with that which exists, any real existence?

Some philosophers say time is purely a conception of the human mind. Others say that time is a form of space, and that space is a form of time. At first sight almost unthinkable, we do find space and time translatable or transmutable, the one into the other, to some extent. Thus, a man may walk a mile in twenty minutes. On a horse he can make it in four minutes. On a motorcycle or auto he may cover his mile in fifty seconds. Light goes a mile in the 186,000th part of a second. Thought flits from any one place to any other place, no matter how distant, in no appreciable time. We can think of down-town, or the moon, or the most distant star, in the same elapsed time.

The smallest instant of time which the human senses can appreciate varies with the sense. The senses are all coarse; two touches on the skin which are the fiftieth of a second apart appear simultaneous. Sounds which come to the ear faster than sixteen to the second merge and become a musical note. The eye accepts sixteen pictures per second on the screen as one continuous picture.

If man could travel with the speed of light, he could, to his own satisfaction, be in two places at the same time; he could spend alternate hundredths of a second here, and a mile from here, and make the journey a hundred and eighty-six times in the second. He could hear, see, smell, taste and touch things in both places at once! We know a man may be in two different *times* in the same *place*. If a man could travel at the speed of light and thus, to his senses, be in two places at one and the same time, then space and time would be dissimilar forms of the same thing!

It is only upon some such hypothesis, that space and time are different aspects of one whole, that the human mind is able to grasp either space, as it seems to us it must be, or time. We can conceive of neither beginning nor ending of either space or time. If time began, once, what was before it? If space ends, somewhere, what is beyond it? We measure our conception of time by the world's movement in space. We measure the miles of space by the time of light-travel through it. If each is measurable in terms of the other, if each is but an aspect of the other, then infinity of either becomes a conception, even if not an understandable one, since we can imagine space merging into time at the " jumping-off place" and time turning into space "at the beginning."

These speculations have been set down here, not to tease the reader's mind, but to give him some small idea of how much there is in that one small symbol of a point within a circle. Like space and time, the circle has neither beginning nor ending. Like the point in the center of the circle, we must be in the center of both space and time, for if we were anywhere else than at the center, we would have to be "nearer" to the "edge of space" and "further" from "the beginning of time;" and such concepts are not possible to the human mind.

The simple symbol, then, becomes the insignia of the vastest mystery we know; it touches our conception of Deity, Who has neither beginning nor ending. It takes our little finite minds upon a great journey into the infinite. It speaks to our hearts of the utter inconceivability of that which is boundless . . . as the love of the Great Architect for us, his children, is boundless.

Many of Freemasonry's symbols have meanings which the mind may grasp; they teach truths which we can understand, and live by. This, the point within a circle, speaks to us of a Something Beyond, because it symbolizes that which we cannot understand. He is a wise initiate who will study it, who will ponder it, and who never will rest content until his efforts to get at its ultimate truth are stopped by the limits of human understanding.

And there are those who say that Freemasonry is "only another secret society!"

PASSED

11 – Manhood

MEN live their lives in the three dimensions of space, which are those of common experience. The scientist, by analogy, can predict the existence of a fourth dimension of space, explain easily some otherwise non-explainable facts of chemistry and physics, but, lacking experimental proof, is not ready to vouch for the existence of the fourth dimension. The mathematician makes no distinction between the three dimensions we know and a fourth, or fifth or any other dimension.

Men live their mental lives in three dimensions; too many of them are bounded by labor, pleasure and health. Ministers of the gospel, Rabbis of the Jewish faith, Priests of Mohammed and the art of Freemasonry teach of another mental dimension; and we explain with ease, by reference to ethics, beliefs and faiths, those phenomena of altruism, charity, brotherly love and the quest of knowledge, which are otherwise mysterious.

But to some few it is given, as to the mathematician and his multitudinous dimensions, to put no limit to the direction in which thought may wander. Such "mental mathematics" consider no one philosophy, but an infinity of philosophies, all true, but each extending further than its predecessor extends. To those so gifted, there is no one music, no one literature, no one poetry, no one system of right and wrong, but an infinity of such systems, each to be explored.

And if you ask, "Who are so gifted?" learn that the answer is as simple as the subject is profound – they are those to whom the Magi have given the gift of gifts – even the gift of imagination.

The Fellowcraft Degree is a system of truths of which we can grasp only the beginning if we look at it with the eyes of a mind, which sees in three dimensions only. But if we look through imagination we can see the infinite possibilities of its complete understanding.

To witness the Fellowcraft Degree without applying to it the magic of an awakened and vivid imagination is to miss its most subtle points and most glorious instruction.

The modern Fellowcraft Degree is, as a whole, emblematic of manhood; to attain is to be "grown up," Masonically speaking. As the Entered Apprentice Degree speaks of birth and babyhood, of first beginnings and first principles, so does the Fellowcraft Degree speak of growth, of strength and of virility, to those who have inward and spiritual ears with which to hear.

Some dispute this; they contend that as the Sublime Degree is the flower and fruit of Freemasonry, it only can be regarded as a culmination. But they mistake, for the Fellowcraft Degree was once the culmination of the degrees of Freemasonry; perhaps it is more truthful to say that Freemasonry had at one time but two degrees, the second of which was the completion of the story.

Today a man grows up, Masonically, in his Fellowcraft Degree. In his Master Mason Degree, he becomes a Master; that is, better informed than the man who is merely "grown up." In the analogy, which sees the three degrees as emblematical of human life, the Master Mason Degree are of old age, a well-spent life, and the hope of a glorious immortality. The Master Mason Degree is no longer a preparation for a human life; it is a preparation for another life. To the Fellowcraft Degree, then, is given the important part of preparing a man, Masonically, for grown Masonic manhood.

In many respects the Fellowcraft Degree is more modern than either the preceding or the succeeding degree. We find in it the strong influence of those men who labored with such enthusiasm immediately following the formation of the Grand Lodge of England in 1717; men who were bound to make their impress felt upon the renewed and revivified society which, following the easy customs of an inexact time, had been more or less casual and without central government.

To understand the degree and what it attempts to do, one must have some knowledge of its history, and of William Preston, who brought the vigor of a trained mind to bear upon the often hasty and ill-considered lectures with which its progenitors were given. He turned these lectures into the elaborate exposition of the five senses and the seven liberal arts and sciences, which we now have. In Preston's day such an exposition of knowledge was all-inclusive; it is not Preston's fault that he knew nothing of science as we know it; that he knew nothing of medicine or biology or archeology or criticism or electricity, or astronomy in the modern sense. There are those who would substitute for the Prestonian lectures and the Prestonian-Webb form of the degree, a wholly modern exposition of the obtaining of knowledge. But should they have their way, the Craft would lose much; our Fellowcraft Degree is hallowed with age, and it is a lovely thing to do as have done all those good brothers and fellows who have gone this way before us.

But there is nothing to prevent us from reading the degree symbolically. We do not have to accept it as literal, any more than we have to accept the first verse of the seventh Chapter of Revelations: *"And after these things I saw four angels standing on the four corners of the earth . . ."* as proof that the earth is square and not round. We can consider the meaning of the degree, and govern ourselves accordingly.

William Preston was more or less discredited for a time by his Masonic compeers, but his labors have remained of use to his brethren long after the bitterness and the jealousies he aroused have been forgotten.

Preston wrote and labored in an era of formalism; the years of the 18th century were those of court and etiquette, of manners raised to the nth power; of conduct rigorously prescribed. The very language of the Fellowcraft Degree, as we know it (somewhat altered by Webb and others), is that of a bygone century, with all its tribute to authority in its manners, all its belief in the power of form to accomplish that which sense and context might fail to do.

No thoughtful man can avoid the impression that this degree is an attempt to emphasize the vital need of knowledge; to encourage study and research, to bring out the beauty of wisdom. It is true that the liberal education, which the degree was, once supposed to outline and encourage is no longer either liberal or educational in fact; but it is still symbolical of all that a good Mason should learn.

The seven liberal arts and sciences are not to us, any more, even the skeleton of a liberal education. Grammar and rhetoric are no longer the important studies they were in 1717. Music is less important, in an age where all the emphasis is put upon making a living and laying up material possessions and wealth, than in 1717, when grace of living was essential. But if we consider these, to Preston, essentials of a "liberal education" as symbolic (as we will see later) we find in the essence of the Fellowcraft Degree, not merely an outworn attempt to provide knowledge and make of the lodge a college, but a powerful symbol, the proper interpretation of which must make a student of any true Freemason, and cause a hunger for fact and theory which will make of him a much greater and more powerful factor in the body politic than his uninstructed neighbor.

The Fellowcraft Degree as a whole is a symbol of manhood; of that pursuit of knowledge, that striving after learning, that inherent wish to know, which marks man as different from the brutes, having a right to raise his eyes heavenwards; aye, even to pry boldly into the mysteries of the space beyond which, only one knows how many infinities of miles away, man seeks for God.

12 – The Master's Piece

BEFORE an initiate may become a Fellowcraft it is demanded of him that he become proficient in the work of the Entered Apprentice Degree, that he learn "by heart" a certain portion of the ritual, and make himself competent to "stand and deliver" it on occasion.

Such a memorization is our sole survival of that ancient custom of Operative Masonry of demanding from the Apprentice, who had served the legal time, usually seven years, a Master's Piece; an example of ability in Masonry by which his fellows could judge whether or not he had made good use of his time and was fit to be "passed" from the state of being but an Apprentice, to that of being a Fellow (or Companion) of the Craft.

Alas, that our modern Master's Piece is so modest in its required effort! For it takes no one very long, nor does it make much of a drain upon time or patience, to learn the *words* by heart. Lucky is he whose instructor is not content with teaching him the words and their order, but who insists upon instructing as to their meaning and their history. He who understands and follows this degree will want to become an earnest student not only of Masonic knowledge, but also of knowledge in general. For of knowledge and its acquiring is this degree most certainly a teacher; from the time of entry through the West Gate until the finish of the lecture, the Entered Apprentice in the process of being "passed" is instructed, taught, given knowledge and urged that only by knowledge can he hope to achieve complete growth and the final glory of Freemasonry, the Sublime Degree of Master Mason.

The Apprentice must be vouched for as proficient by his instructor, or pass an examination in open lodge as to his ability in the Entered Apprentice Degree. This beautiful custom is sometimes omitted, especially in large lodges in busy centers, where the length of the business meeting and the press of work often seem to make it impossible to take the time for this "examination of a Master's Piece." It is a pity; those lodges not yet too busy, nor too big, to retain this old, old custom may congratulate themselves. The initiate who has to undergo that ordeal, if ordeal it proves, in after years will be glad if he stood on his own feet in front of the Altar and proved himself an able and informed Entered Apprentice before a Lodge of Fellowcraft.

In either case, however, the Apprentice must learn something. We seldom inquire what, if any, knowledge our Apprentices have learned; if they know the words, we are satisfied. Indeed, if we have picked wisely from the world of the profane, we may rest satisfied; no good material out of which a Master Mason can be made will rest content merely with knowing the words. He will want to know the facts, the inner meaning, and the derivation.

But the words he must learn. His Master's Piece he must make, and make it to the satisfaction of the Craft assembled. Here, alas, come hurry and bustle; here come the rush and the roar of the twentieth century. And here, to their shame be it said, come sometimes instructors more interested in "getting their man through" than in being real teachers. Sometimes instructors do not wholly instruct; they "pass" an initiate as fit for the Fellowcraft Degree, who does not know the "work" and could not pass a competent examination before open lodge to save his hurried life!

This is all wrong! Not only is it necessary for a good Mason to know the work of the degree; the learning of that work is in itself a symbol. How, pray, Bro. Instructor, can we expect one we are trying to make a Master Mason, ever to respect and venerate our symbols, if you say to him, in effect, "Oh, you are not really proficient, but you've struggled with the ritual a week of evenings with me, and I guess you'll learn it some day . . . come on in!" Is that the way to impress an initiate with the symbolism of the Master's Piece; the symbol which, translated, reads: "You must serve your time, you must act as a true man, you must prove yourself before your brethren; what we give you is of value, it is priceless, you cannot have it for nothing. We like you, we have lived with you, we have accepted you, but now you come to ask us for a great gift. You must prove yourself worthy. Make your Master's Piece. Put in it all your skill, all your wit, and all your heart; submit it to the judgment of us, your Masters . . . we, as Fellows of the Craft, will judge whether you are fit to be a Fellowcraft, by the way you do an Apprentice's work."

Should an Entered Apprentice read these words, he is most earnestly besought to let them sink in. Learn your work! Learn it well! Don't be satisfied, even if your instructor is satisfied, until *you* know that it has become a part of you. The writer of these words, a Master Mason of many years' standing, and one who loves the gentle Craft, tells you from a heart full of gratitude for all that it has meant to him, that the better you labor upon your Master's Piece, the better you learn your work, the more joy you will have from your Freemasonry. For, after all, it is not only to benefit the Craft as a whole, but also to benefit the individual brother, that he must become proficient. He who regards not this requirement as a symbol, who skimps or slights it, must suffer in denial of opportunity, in failure to appreciate, in loss of precious knowledge, in mental darkness where should be light and understanding.

13 – "Amos, What Seest Thou?"

THUS he shewed me: and, behold, the Lord stood upon a wall made by a plumbline, with a plumbline in his hand. And the Lord said unto me, Amos, what seest thou? And I said, A plumbline. Then said the Lord, Behold, I will set a plumbline in the midst of my people Israel: I will not again pass by them any more.

Every Fellowcraft hears these two verses from the Old Testament Book of Amos, as he passes about the lodge room during his circumambulation. It is somewhat regrettable that, with the laudable intention of introducing a little "color" into the ceremony, lodges frequently have these words sung, either as a solo or by a quartette. Just what the initiate getting his Fellowcraft Degree is supposed to absorb from a song, the words of which he cannot understand, is not stated. It is custom; many lodges do it; the Fellowcraft can find the quotation in the Monitor or the Bible!

However, the reading from Amos did not come into the degree by chance; there is no more real reason for singing it than for singing the obligation or the charge. But, while it seems simple enough, just because it is so often sung, and is so seldom visualized as a symbol, let us examine into it a little.

It is not necessary that we become Bible commentators, or even students, to find both poetry and sonorousness in these words; we do not have to be higher critics nor theologians to interpret the words of the Lord, as reported by Amos, to mean something else than the literal transcript suggests. Leaving to others the question as to whether the Lord spoke to Amos or whether Amos merely thought He did, we can consider what is meant when a Supreme Power stands upon a wall made by a plumbline, takes a plumbline in his hand, and declares intention to set a plumbline among his people, and "not again pass by them any more."

Students will recall that Israel had been having a hard time; pestilence and war, famine and poverty, affliction after affliction, were upon them. Now comes the promise, "I will not again pass by them any more." Why? Because of the plumbline? Hardly. Because, perhaps, they were now fit to be judged by the plumbline!

The writer is no theological student, and prays the pardon of any ministers who may find his interpretation lacking, or impertinence in his attempt. He here considers this quotation, not as an account of an interview with God, but for its Masonic significance.

An operative mason would not use a plumbline to determine whether a wall, tumbling down, were in a state of disrepair. He would know it without any plumbline. Any observer would know it. One does not need a pint cup to measure a river to see if it is one or more gallons in extent; the fact is obvious. A people which exists in a state of anarchy, with its lack of law, murder, theft, revolution, do not need to be judged by a court; the whole world condemns them, as it condemned Russia during the revolution.

But a pint cup may be used to measure a skinful of wine; a judge is needed to determine the merits of a case in which there is some right and some wrong on both sides, and a mason uses a plumbline to determine if the wall he builds is quite straight, or perhaps, if it needs bracing here, or diminishing there.

The Fellowcraft comes among his brethren to be judged by a plumbline. No anarchist, he! He would not be here if he were. He is not "judged" at all, in the sense that his brethren think he is guilty of anything for which punishment is to be meted out. He is judged by the way he learns, the kind of a man he becomes and whether or not he stands up, by the plumbline; whether he moves by the square, and walks upon a level, or if he sags away from the perpendicular, follows a zigzag course and prefers to walk down hill!

"I will not again pass by them any more." That was the Lord's promise to Israel through Amos; having set up a plumbline, and spoken of a plumbline while standing on a plumb wall made plumb by a plumbline; having, in other words, emphasized the means of judgment, the Lord declared his intention not to pass by them any more.

There is not today, and we have no reason to suppose there ever was, an unconditional promise. The condition may not be stated, but it is always implied. It is unthinkable that the Lord could have meant that he would not pass by his people any more if they rejected his plumbline; that no matter how evil they became, he would still use the plumbline in judgment.

So the reading from Amos must be to the Fellowcraft a conditional promise, not an absolute assurance for all time. Freemasonry makes no promises that she cannot keep. She makes none that she does not keep. But, sometimes, alas, a brother makes promises to her that he does not keep!

And when that happens, the plumbline is withdrawn. It is no longer that undeviating standard of judgment of the perfectly erect, the mere use of which is an assurance that those who use it find in the material to be measured that which is nearly perfect and upright!

Throughout all the degrees the insistence is upon square, level, compasses, trowel, gauge; all tools for making stones fit to use in a temple. In the Fellowcraft Degree we have also the plumb, or plumbline, used not only in dressing rough ashlars to perfect ashlars but also in making walls. The Lord stood on a wall made by a plumbline; Amos gave to us for all time the right way of making a wall true and upright. So the plumbline of Masonic significance is to be used by the Fellowcraft in making his wall true and upright.

None may escape judgment by pleading "but I have no plumbline; I do not know how to use a plumbline." For every man has a plumbline in his heart; if the cord is twisted, the plumb broken, the whole awry, Freemasonry will set another in its place. To fear and love God; to walk uprightly before all men; to bend the attentive ear to the instructive tongue; to go out of one's way to serve a brother; to be helpful, kind, considerate, tolerant, charitable, and wise; to learn, to teach, to follow the Golden Rule . . . these are the strands of which Freemasonry weaves her plumbline, and when the cord is woven and weighted with the plumb of intellect to pull it straight, any man, be his education never so limited or his vision never so clouded, can see whether or not he measures upright enough to be worthy to be judged by its perfection.

14 – Spurious

THAT there are spurious Masons in the world is not a Masonic secret. One method of their detection, so the ritual informs us, is to be found in the Fellowcraft Degree; it is secret. Modern Freemasonry is "regular" when it can trace its descent through dispensation or charter or warrant back to the Mother Grand Lodge, or to a legalization by that Grand Lodge or one of its subsidiary Provincial Grand Lodges, or some other Grand Lodge which in its turn was regular, following the reconciliation of 1813.

Masonry is irregular, or clandestine, when it traces its descent to other and not "regular" Grand Bodies.

This may seem, to the Masonic student, a somewhat cursory way of approaching what is well recognized to be a most difficult subject; it avoids all reference to Masonry made "irregular" by the withdrawing of friendly relations of a Grand Lodge, as for instance, certain French Masonry is deemed irregular by practically all English-speaking Grand Lodges.

But the point to be made here is not one of history, nor even of fact, but of the symbolism to be discovered in the spurious Mason and the Fellowcraft means by which he may be detected.

For the literal-minded Mason, it will come as a shock, perhaps, to read that many of his brethren put but little reliance upon the test. Yet it would be idle to insist upon it as a practical Masonic measure. No well instructed examination committee would condemn a visitor as a "spurious Mason" merely because he inverted the Fellowcraft test. If they knew him to be a member of a "regular lodge" and in good standing, and he was well instructed otherwise, failure here would not condemn him. Nor should it; for with all the Masons in the world, with all the renegades who have come and gone, with all the "exposés" of Masonry which have been made, it would be absurd to predicate "regularity" or "clandestinism" upon some ritual test.

Either we retain this in the ritual because it has a "covered" meaning, keeping it merely as we do our vermiform appendix, until necessity bids us cut it out; or we are a foolish set of men aping the old merely because it is old.

The words themselves indicate a "covered" meaning. We are told that by doing thus and such we may "the more readily" detect the spurious Mason. We are not told that this is an absolute test; merely that it is an assistance.

In the olden days when Freemasonry was much simpler, much smaller, and perhaps much more select than it is now; in days when Freemasons were few and their secrets hard to come by; such a test might readily have been practical as well as theoretical. Today it has little practical value as a test, but much as an instruction. For there are "spurious" Masons in the world, even among Masons made such in "regular" lodges. One can conceive an innocently made clandestine Mason . . . one who believed he was applying to, and receiving the degrees from, a regular lodge . . . becoming a very good Mason. And any of us can see, without going very far, many a regularly made Mason who is wholly "spurious" in all that he says and does, Masonically. The membership committee of the lodge is not always composed of the wisest and best men in the lodge. It does not always do its work thoroughly. And even the wisest and best of men, doing work thoroughly, may make a mistake. So that, at times, we gain material in our lodge only in a sense to lose; the material is poor, the Masonic product almost nil. The result is a "spurious" Mason. Reference is not made here to the "poor Mason." There are men too busy to cultivate Masonry. There are practical, hard-headed, soft-hearted, busy, charitable, excellent men who never read anything, who never think anything, who never do anything, but work and play; who never come to lodge, who seldom do anything Masonic, unasked; yet who will heed the call of brotherhood and work to the limit at its behest. One could not call them "spurious" because they never heard of Anderson, or cannot tell whether a Royal Arch Chapter belongs to the York or Scottish Rite!

The real "spurious Mason" is he to whom the Craft makes no sentimental appeal; the man for whom Masonry is "all business," and who, therefore, thinks of a "brotherhood" as but a passing fancy.

If this were a perfect world there would be no need for Freemasonry. If all men were perfect, what could Freemasonry do for mankind? It is, therefore, no slander on her fair fame, that she is deserted by a few of her followers, that some embrace her only to turn away. Perhaps Freemasonry knew this from the beginning, and so pointed out, in that very quiet and softly touching way of hers, how we should "the more readily" detect those who were not truly of her beliefs.

He will be a wise Fellowcraft who makes it his business to be in all ways a regular Fellowcraft. When he is, he will know the "spurious" Mason as readily as the doctor knows the diseased from the healthy.

A man wise in the ways of the world and of Masons, one who has held every honor within the gift of the Craft, aye, even to the Grand East, once told a young Fellowcraft just passed: "When you see a Mason with his button on his coat and think, 'What can he do for me?' you may know yourself a spurious Mason. But when on seeing the emblem you think, 'What may I do for my brother?' you may know yourself well on the way to be wholly 'regular'."

This, then, is the practical test; this, then, is the covered meaning in the Fellowcraft ceremony by which we may discover who is spurious and who really "of us": that we examine, not his mind, but his heart; that we look, not for words, but for feelings; that we judge, not by knowledge, but by intent. If he is selfish, self-seeking, an egotist, wholly wrapped up in himself, he is a "spurious" Mason; aye, though he have every degree and every jewel in Freemasonry.

And if he be unselfish, so that the call of brotherhood makes him go on swiftly running feet to help, aid and assist his brethren in their distress, then he is a "regular" Mason; aye, though he has forgotten his ritual and seldom or never comes to lodge.

For that is brotherhood . . . and true Freemasonry is the practice of brotherhood.

15 – "With Winding Stairs"

AN outstanding symbol in the Fellowcraft Degree is the flight of Winding Stairs. In the Book of Kings we find, "they went up with winding stairs into the middle chamber." We go up "with winding stairs" into "The Middle Chamber of King Solomon's Temple." Also we travel up a winding stairs of life, to arrive, if we climb steadfastly, at the middle chamber of existence, which is removed from birth, babyhood and youth by the steps of knowledge and experience, but which is not so high above the ground that we are not as yet of the earth, earthy; not so high that we can justifiably regard it as more than a Stepping-Off Place from which we may, perhaps, ascend to the Sanctum Sanctorum; that holy of holies, in which our troubled spirits find rest, and our eyes see God.

There is a symbolism in the fact that the stairway winds. A straight stairway is not so easy to climb as a winding one, which, because of the fact that it does wind, ascends by easier stages than one which rises as a ladder. Yet, a straight stairway has the goal constantly in sight; while it may be more difficult in the effort and strength required, it is easier in that one can see where one is going. There is no faith needed in climbing a ladder; we can visualize the top and have its inspiration constantly before us as we rise rung after rung.

But the winding stairway is one which tries a man's soul. He *must* believe, or he cannot reach the top. Nothing is clear before him but the next step. He must take it on faith that there is a top, that if he but climb long enough he will indeed reach a Middle chamber, a goal, a place of light. In such a way are the Winding Stairs and the Middle Chamber symbols of life and manhood. No man knows what he will become; as a boy he may have a goal, but may reach another Middle Chamber than that he visualized as he started the ascent. No man knows whether he will ever climb all the stairs; the Angel of Death may stand but around the turn on the next step. Yet in spite of a lack of knowledge of what is at the top of the stairs, in spite of the fact that a Flaming Sword may bar his ascent, man climbs. He climbs in faith that there is a goal and that he will reach it; and no good Freemason doubts but that for those who never see the glory of the Middle Chamber in his life, a lamp is set that they may see still farther in another, better life.

We are taught that we should use the five senses to climb the remaining seven steps of the stairway, which are the seven liberal arts and sciences. Again we must remember that William Preston, who put so practical an interpretation upon these steps, lived in an age when these did, indeed, represent all of knowledge. But we must not refuse to grow because the ritual has not grown with modern discovery. When we rise by Grammar and Rhetoric, we must consider that they mean not only language, but all methods of communication. The step of Logic means a knowledge not only of a method of reasoning, but of all reasoning which logicians have accomplished. When we ascend by Arithmetic and Geometry, we must visualize all science; since science is but measurement, in the true mathematical sense, it requires no great stretch of the imagination to read into these two steps all that science may teach. The step denominated Music means not only sweet and harmonious sounds, but all beauty–poetry, art, nature, loveliness of whatever kind. Not to be familiar with the beauty which nature provides, is to be, by so much, less a man; to stunt, by so much, a striving soul. As for the seventh step of Astronomy, surely it means not only the study of the solar system and the stars, as it did in William Preston's day, but also the study of all that is beyond the earth; of spirit and the world of spirit, of ethics, philosophy, the abstract . . . of Deity.

Preston built better than he knew; his seven steps are both logical in arrangement and suggestive in their order. The true Fellowcraft will see in them a guide to the making of a man rich in mind and spirit, by which riches only can the truest brotherhood be practiced.

The Fellowcraft Degree is one of action. Recall where you wore your cable tow; but think not that it confines action; it urges it. A great authority has stated that the words come from the Hebrew, and mean, in effect, "his pledge." Here, then, "his pledge" is for action, for a doing, a girding up, an effort to be made. What effort? To climb, to rise! How? By the use of the five senses to take in and make knowledge apart of the mind and heart. What knowledge? All knowledge!

Conceived thus, the Fellowcraft Degree, from being a mere ceremony, a stepping stone from the Entered Apprentice Degree to that of the Master, becomes something sublime; it is emblematic of the struggle of life, not materially, but spiritually, a symbol with high hope and encouragement constantly held forth. There *is* a Middle Chamber; the steps *do* lead somewhere; man can climb them if he will. Not for the drone, the laggard, the journeyer by the easy paths upon the level, but for the fighter, the adventurer, the man with courage and a stout heart, is this degree of Freemasonry. The Fellowcraft must be of high courage, for that which is not worth working for and fighting for is not worth having. It is no easy journey that we make through life, and it is no easy journey that we make through the mazes of this degree. In its Middle Chamber lecture are profound philosophies, deep truths, great facts concealed. He who is a true Fellowcraft will study these for himself; he will not be content with the Prestonian lecture as an end; it will be to him but a means.

For thousands of years men saw the rainbow and the best they could do was call it a promise of God. So indeed it may be to us all, but it is also a manifestation of beauty in nature. It is caused by the operation of well understood laws, and when artificially produced in the spectroscope, it is the key with which we unlocked the mysteries of the heavens. For as long as man has lived upon this earth the lightning flashed and the thunder roared to no end but terror and beauty. In the last few hundred years man has read the first part of the mysterious story of electricity and taken for himself the power

God put in nature. Had man been content merely with what he saw and heard he would still be as ignorant as the beasts of the field.

So should the mysteries of the Fellowcraft be to the initiate. The degree is but a great symbol, given in one evening, of all that a man may make of his life. It is a lamp to guide the feet, not, as Preston would have had it, both the feet and the path. Preston and his brethren were Speculative Masons, indeed; but we are enlightened as he never was. If we fail to use the light he lit, or see by its radiance a higher climb, and a Greater Stairway than ever he visualized, the fault is within us, and not in our opportunity.

There are thousands who pass through this degree who see in it only a ceremony, just as there are thousands who see in the rainbow only color in the sky, thousands who see a lightning flash but as a portent of danger. But the thoughtful man sees in the Winding Stairs an invitation, an urge to climb, to learn, to know, to reach that Middle Chamber of life from which one can look back on an effort well made, a life well spent, a goal well won; and then forward . . . to what awaits in the final degree. For the Sublime Degree of Master Mason is a symbol, too . . . perhaps the greatest symbol man has ever made for himself to point a way up a yet greater Winding Stairs to a higher vaulted Upmost Chamber, where the real Master Mason, raised from a Fellowcraft, may reach up as a little child and touch the hand of God.

16 – Tools

NOT how many, but how few laws and regulations, is Freemasonry's idea of government. A Mason is trusted; he is expected to make the existing laws all inclusive, not to interpret them in a narrow and literal fashion. Helping the needy is to be done as far as possible "without injury to yourself or family." He is required to express a belief in Deity . . . not some particular Deity. His "regular attendance" is expected, but not when it interferes with his regular vocation. Everywhere we find the spirit of toleration, and of leaving to self-respect and good faith the interpretation of Freemasonry's laws, regulations and requirements.

The same toleration applies in the interpretation of symbolism. There are certain symbols the meaning of which is explained in words almost of one syllable; but no prohibition stops anyone who may find another and better meaning in addition to the one elaborated in the ritual. The working tools of a Fellowcraft, plumb, square and level, are explained thus: "The plumb admonishes us to walk uprightly in our several stations before God and man, squaring our actions by the square of virtue, and remembering that we are travelling upon the level of time to that 'undiscovered country, from whose bourne no traveler returns.'" But there is nothing in the Monitor or the ritual of the degree which prevents us from finding our own interpretations of those symbols.

It is not difficult to see that a plumb may have other symbolic meanings than an admonishment to "walk uprightly." To "walk uprightly" is a phrase which in itself may have a dozen meanings. It can hardly refer to physical posture. Neither can it refer to locomotion; the admonition would mean as much in the moral sense if we were told to stand uprightly or run uprightly. "Uprightly" of course refers to our passage through life. But the plumb may do more than so admonish us. It may be that symbol by which we erect our thoughts; for there is crooked thinking as well as crooked building. Masons know that buildings must stand straight up if they are to endure, but "straight" is not in itself an absolute term. The Washington Monument and the Eiffel Tower are not parallel; each is "plumb" only to sea level in its own location. To an observer far from the earth these two "plumb" structures rise from the surface of the globe at a considerable angle.

Thus we can easily read into "plumb" not only the teaching of straight thinking, but toleration. What is "straight" to one may not be straight to another; as geographic location alters the perspective of what is "straight," so our position in the world of thought may alter our ideas of what is "straight" thinking. Two men may have vastly different ideas of what Truth is, yet each may be right from his own standpoint. A plumb which admonishes us to recognize that, to an observer afar off . . . to the Great Architect, for instance . . . both thoughts may be right, even if different, is a symbol with a concealed meaning well worthstudy.

We speak of the "square of virtue." Virtue is, literally, a "disposition to conform cordially to the requirements of the moral law." More specifically, *it* is the moral law. But what is the moral law?

Ideas of morality change with time, and with geographical location. A thousand years ago boiling a criminal in oil was considered a perfectly moral act on the part of the law. Two thousand years further back, and "an eye for an eye" was held to be the right standard. Then One came who brought anew law . . .

It is neither moral nor legal in the western world to have more than one wife or husband. But in Turkey and Polynesia it is perfectly moral to have several.

Time and custom, location and ideas, alter conceptions of the moral law for some acts and thoughts, yet certain "squares of virtue" are the same for all mankind. No matter where we live, or of what race we are, no matter what religion we profess or to what country we belong, it is the opposite of virtuous to steal, to bear false witness, to murder, to betray one's country. But Freemasonry is not concerned with the major crimes when she bids an initiate obey the moral law; if she supposed a man was a potential thief, murderer, liar or traitor, she would never admit him to her ranks. It is the moral law but partly expressed, or unexpressed, in the written law, to which she refers.

As the operative mason had each his individual square, so have we, each of us, our own individual square of virtue. But the operative masons must of necessity have had squares which were alike in their "squareness." If their squares differed, then their stones would not be alike and the wall they made would not be plumb and level.

It is not difficult to believe that operative masons might well have been allowed some latitude as to the *size* of their squares, of the *materials* out of which they were made. Some might prefer a square with one long and one short side; others might want them with sides of equal length. Some might do better work with squares of steel, while yet others preferred squares of wood. But it is not thinkable that they were allowed any latitude in the angle of their squares; all had to be ninety degrees.

With speculative Masons, the *kind* of square we use as the square of virtue will be dictated by what manner of men we are. And as there is room for an honest difference of opinion regarding many things, there is room for differing squares of virtue. "In the most friendly manner remind him of his faults" does not mean that we are to judge our neighbor, who builds with a square of steel, because we prefer to build with a square of wood. But when he builds with a square which is out of true, *then* it is time for us to "whisper good counsel in his ear."

The moral law, then, to which Masons must conform, must be considered to be that general body of public opinion, as recognized by us all; it is by this that we must try our squares of virtue. If our individual tools conform to this standard, then we may use them fearlessly, and have them of such size of mental material as our education and our powers of thinking permit.

The level is an instrument used by operative masons to run horizontals. Like the perpendiculars, all horizontals are not parallel to each other. The base of the Capitol at Washington and the base of the Woolworth building in New York could not, if continued at the same levels until they met, meet upon a level. Each is level for its own latitude, only. So that, if we are admonished to walk uprightly and by the square of virtue on that level of time on which we also travel, we have at least a dialectic right to consider that each of us has his own level of time. We share a common time, in that we are all alive at the same time, and that year, month and day is the same for us all (not to break the argument with consideration of travel about the globe and the "lost day" at the 180th meridian). But in the larger sense, none of us travels the same level of time. To some of us life is short and swift, and the days pass almost like the flapping of a mighty wing. To others, less fortunate in vivid perception, in interest or gladness in our work, days are long and slow, life is long, long; almost too long. Such "times" are surely not the same.

It is seen, therefore, that even such objective symbols as square, level and plumb, with an explanation and a definition printed in the manual, are not without possibilities of individual interpretation. Of course, by this very argument, the reader's interpretations are as good in theory, and may be far better in practice, than those given here, which are the writer's. But it is not so important that one make the very *best* individual interpretation as that one make *some* individual interpretation; what a man thinks is usually far less important in individual development, in education and in progress along the mental level, than that he does think! For the man who thinks awry may be taught, or learn of himself to think aright. But he who thinks never . . . for him there is no hope, save as there is always hope of the witless sheep that they will, somehow, come home!

By the plumb, stand, walk, run. By the square, which has been tried by and fitted to the moral law, try actions and thoughts to see if they fit ninety degrees of honor and candor and honesty and nobility of soul. Be not satisfied to travel on a level; there are too many levels for that. Insist that the level be a true one for the place and station occupied. For so, and only so, may we use the working tools of a Fellowcraft wisely. Not all do so; too many are well satisfied with five lines in a Monitor and "pass on to the next station." But the great hope for Freemasonry in this generation is the fact that the number who insist on doing their own thinking is increasing. Those "Fellows of the Craft" who want their own plumbs, squares and levels to compare with their neighbors', instead of being content all with one set of tools in the Masters' hands, are rapidly on the increase.

17 – Rough and Perfect

A SIGN or character with only one meaning is not a symbol, but a fact. A closed hand with one finger pointing, may easily be a symbol; but if mounted upon a post and set by the side of a path, it is no longer a symbol; it is a fact, a mere character indicating direction.

The Rough and Perfect Ashlars in a lodge have seemed to many to be less symbols than facts; the Rough Ashlar, a stone from the quarry in its unfinished state, is so obviously the applicant for the degrees; the Perfect Ashlar, the result of "good work, true work, square work," is so obviously the initiated Freemason; that many writers on symbolism pass these over with but little explanation, apparently thinking that but little is needed.

But, as has been said before and probably will be again in this little attempt to make clearer some of the hidden meanings in Freemasonry's vast treasure house of symbols, many of them have both obvious meanings and covered meanings.

The Rough Ashlar, while but an unfinished stone from the quarry , is not a stone merely found, picked up, happened upon. It is a stone tooled out of the quarry. Some work has been done upon it. It has been selected. It is apparently a good stone; there is nothing which can be said against it, and something may be said for it, else it were not taken from the quarry and brought to the Fellow of the Craft by the Apprentice, for the former to work upon it with his tools.

So are our initiates; they are not men merely happened upon, picked up; some work has been done upon them. They have been examined. Questions have been asked about them. They appear to be good material. The lodge is willing to accept them as such, pending further work. Here is found a real Masonic reason for the unwritten Masonic law, that Freemasonry "does not seek." For if she sought, she would the more easily take, from among the ranks of those among whom she sought, men not tested; men not examined; men not outwardly flawless.

It is easy to pick holes in such a reading of the symbolism and say "but no rough ashlar ever offered itself to the workmen." Of course, stones do not offer themselves, but neither do stones build themselves; nay, nor square themselves. If the Rough Ashlar is material for the Perfect Ashlar, so is the initiate the material out of which the Fellowcraft may be made.

The Perfect Ashlar is made from the Rough Ashlar entirely by a process of taking away; not of adding to. It is not in the power of the Fellowcraft to add anything material to his Rough Ashlar. All he can do to it is chip, chip, chip away the rough edges, the sharp places, the visible flaws. In other words, the Perfect Ashlar, if it exists at all in any stone, is there all the time; to get at it requires but patient work. So, indeed, may there be many objects inside a stone; the most beautiful statue is already in the rough piece of marble from which it is carved. All the workman needs to do is knock away the marble which is not a part of the statue, and there it is! Yet how few the artists who can do the work!

Not many operators can hew a Rough Ashlar into a Perfect Ashlar. The Perfect Ashlar is there, undoubtedly. But it takes rare skill to "knock away the unwanted stone." This, perhaps, accounts for the fact that there are so few Perfect Ashlars in a lodge! Few doubt that within all men is the perfect piece of work; are we not told that man is made in God's image? But so covered is he with roughnesses, so encrusted with sharp points, so hard is the stone and so dull the tools, that most of us, whether we hew upon another Rough Ashlar or upon our own, fail to produce perfection.

If the Perfect Ashlar exists only as a symbol, and never in this world as that which is symbolized, why have it at all? And here we come to the covered meaning! The Perfect Ashlar is not only a symbol, but an idea; it is not only an example of what may be done, but the inspiration to try to do it. Because one may never win the race is no reason for not running! Because one may never solve the problem is no reason for not trying. "He builds too low, who builds beneath the stars" is not a complaint that man has not yet erected a House unto High Heaven; merely an admonition that one can try, regardless of how ill he succeeds.

All of Freemasonry, from the preparation of the initiate in the ante-room to the laying away with the Sprig of Acacia and the Lambskin Apron of the Master Mason in the "narrow house appointed for all living," is a striving after something better. If, anywhere within Freemasonry, perfection could be attained, Freemasonry would have no further mission. So the Perfect Ashlar is much more than a symbol of material which has been squared; it is a symbol of the idea, the unattainable, the perfection for which man must strive, even though he knows his striving cannot be crowned with success. The workman who labors on the Rough Ashlar may never get it perfectly to fit the square, or stand absolutely erect by the plumb. But he learns the art while striving, and thus his striving is not in vain.

No perfect piece of stone was ever yet set in any building. Yet buildings stand erect, and perfect. Here we get a hint of that wonderful law of compensation, the workings of which are everywhere to be seen, and never yet understood. If my stone is less than perfect, so, too, is yours. Yet yours and mine, and a thousand other stones, each in its way falling short of perfection, balance imperfection against imperfection and make a perfect wall. In some such way, perhaps, The Great Architect erects a perfect structure out of faulty humanity; where I am evil, you are good; where I am selfish, you are generous; where I am weak, you are strong, and together we make a course in the Unseen Temple Not Made with Hands, which is fit for the Master Builder.

These, then, are the covered meanings of the Ashlars; and if the Rough Ashlar seem more of the earth, earthy, and therefore more familiar, more easy to live with, even more loveable, linger not too long over it. For just beyond is the Perfect Ashlar, at once a symbol and an inspiration. If it speaks at all beyond its elementary meaning, surely it beckons onward and upward, towards a height we may not see . . . a light too bright for mortal eyes.

18 – Choose

No symbols in the Blue Lodge have a greater antiquity in written records, than the two columns between which pass every initiate.

The initiate passes between them on his way into a symbolic lodge for the first time; he does not see them, and no reference is made to them in the Entered Apprentice Degree, but they are there, nevertheless. It is not until after he receives his Fellowcraft obligation, and is thus in effect a Fellowcraft of his lodge, that the initiate is led between the columns and shown them, being offered at the same time some explanations which, too often, fail to explain.

But the fault, if fault there is, is not in the system or the philosophy, but in the mind of the initiate, which is willing to accept half truths, partial light, dim hints, when by a little reading and study he might receive more light that he can use!

For these ancient symbols have many meanings, and each one leads to another, larger, farther off, harder to understand, and therefore more worth the winning.

Both the II Book of Chronicles, and the I Book of Kings refer to the two columns in the porch of the Temple of King Solomon; dimensions are given, and the names are set forth, but you shall look in vain in Old Testament or New for any explanation of why the columns were there or what they meant.

From the translation of the Hebrew names Jachin and Boaz, Masons have said that they mean "In Strength He shall Establish His Kingdom." But earnest students have pointed out that the Hebrew words are susceptible of more than one translation, and that it requires no great stretch of a translator's imagination to make the names mean "in wisdom is there power."

Albert Pike, the great Masonic symbolist, finds so many meanings in the two columns that even an abstract of his

words about them would more than fill the space which may
be given to them here. Perhaps it is as well; symbols usually
have more power for him who can read their meaning for
himself than for those who must depend upon another's
reading.

The world about us shows a continual struggle, and a
continual effort to arrive at an equilibrium. Evil and good,
strength and weakness, selfish egotism and humanitarianism,
centrifugal and centripetal forces, are continually in
opposition; in a balance between them is there a state of rest.

One column on the porch of the Temple meant strength;
strength does not mean mere physical muscle, however. The
whole of Solomon's life, his every act and move, show him to
have been one who revered the spiritual side of life. His
wisdom, his wise judging, his building of the Temple, his
leadership, were all concerned with other things than mere
brute force. Is it, then, difficult to conceive of Boaz, usually
translated merely "strength" being here used to mean wisdom,
knowledge, learning, rather than muscle, brute force, power
of the arm?

More than one Masonic philosopher has chosen so to
translate it. Nowhere in Freemasonry is there a triumph of
matter over mind. Nowhere in Freemasonry is combat, army,
struggle of man with man, exalted above the spiritual. Always,
in the end, that which is within, unseen, belonging to the divine
in man, is brought to the ascendent over the mere physical. It
seems both reasonable and consistent for Speculative Masons
to read one of the meanings of the two columns as "By wisdom
shall the kingdom be established."

The initiate passes between the pillars; not by, nor around,
but *between*. The original columns were upon the "porch" of
the Temple of King Solomon. "Porch" does not mean an
excrescence in front of the Temple upon which men sat to get
the air. It means (Hebrew, *ulam*) an arch; it means (Greek,
pulon) a gateway. It means (Greek, *proaulion*) a vestibule. It
means, (Greek, *stoa*) a standing place. In the Bible, all these
words occur, with these several meanings; according to good

authority it is as "arch" that the word "porch" is to be interpreted. Thus we have two columns supporting an arch before the Temple. And an arch is made either to support something above; or to pass under, to get into something beyond.

Lodges have no arch above the columns. For thousands of years man has erected his monoliths as a symbol of Deity, nor thought it necessary to connect them by an arch. Whether or not Solomon had columns supporting an arch (or porch) need not trouble us. What does concern us is that we pass between strength or wisdom, an establishment or a process of making . . . in other words, we are, ourselves, at the point of balance between two forces.

For power, whether it be that of mere brute strength or great knowledge, can be used for evil as well as for good; that which is established by strength is not necessarily good because it is strong. Freemasonry seems to tell us here that there is neither inherent good nor inherent evil in wisdom; that the power to make, by means of wisdom, may be used for evil as well as for good. Fire is a wonderful servant; a poor master. Fire is neither evil nor good; it is our use of it which is evil or good. Dynamite may blow up a church full of little children, learning of God; or it may blast away the fallen mine and release a hundred men otherwise condemned to a hideous death. The dynamite is neither evil nor good; it is our use of it which is evil or good.

So with our columns; one represents strength, knowledge, power; the other, the ability to use the power. We are led neither to one side nor to the other. We pass not by, nor around, but between. We are urged to observe neither to the exclusion of the other. We are free agents; moral forces may move us to use our knowledge for our brethren; selfish forces may urge us to establish our kingdom by our strength regardless of what happens to the other man's kingdom.

The choice is ours. Freemasonry's teachings show us why and how our choice should be made. The Master Mason Degree holds the secret of the reward of a life well spent. But here, in the midst of the Fellowcraft Degree, which is of manhood, we come to the choice, to the place where the roads fork; and if we read not the symbolism of the two columns aright, if we pass between them without thought, and get from that passage no lesson of what and how and why we can do as a free man must, choose . . . then, indeed, are these great symbols lost upon us; and we the poorer that we have not made our own the beauty to be found in this deep and beautiful degree.

19 – Fear

A MASTER Mason who is afraid to face the truth is not a good Master Mason!

In all three of the Obligations which Entered Apprentice, Fellowcraft and Master Mason take upon themselves, are certain penalties. No man ignorant enough to believe that such penalties ever were, or are now, put into effect by a fraternity which begins in love of God, and ends in patriotism, charity, toleration and education, has any business in Freemasonry.

If the penalties are not to be taken literally, obviously they are symbols, and as such, subject to the same liberal interpretation that other Masonic symbols may have.

So much seems logical. And so does the next step; if penalties literally taken are entirely abhorrent to the gentle teachings of Freemasonry, if they are but a survival of some of the brutal laws of hundreds of years ago, why should they not be expunged from the ritual and their place taken by others, equally as drastic, perhaps, but appealing to our minds and hearts, rather than to our animal fears?

Many have advocated such a course. Yet, as all Freemasons know, the substance of the penalties is preserved in certain ways through all Masonic life; never a lodge meeting that reference is not made to them. They have also the sanction of an antiquity which has succeeded in making even more unusual matters respectable! (If one were addressing any other audience than Freemasons, one would have to apologize for vagueness, but the Master Mason will fully comprehend, and, it is hoped, applaud the discretion here employed!)

A man takes off his hat in the presence of a woman, or to greet a friend, relic of days when he doffed his helmet of steel to show he felt no fear of bodily harm. A man offers his hand to his friend in token of friendliness; it must be the bare hand, without gauntlets protecting it, or weapon concealed in it. A gallant bends low before a woman and kisses the back of her hand; he salutes with bent bare head in token of belief that no blow will descend upon it. A man walks between the woman he escorts and the street; in olden days, curbs were non-existent and the walk merged with the road; if there was mud, it was the man who must walk in it, not the woman.

Yet there is no agitation for a new system of salutation, of greeting, of escort. Our present practices are but pleasant symbols of respect and brotherly feeling, though they had origin in a time when every man was his own keeper and danger lurked on every hand.

The penalties in our obligations, then, are symbols. A Freemason may forswear himself and shout from the housetop every secret he has sworn to keep. He may publish all he knows, and a great deal that he doesn't know, about Freemasonry in a book and hawk it about the streets. He may stand in the market place and hold the fraternity up to ridicule and tell anything, everything, he wishes. Nothing will happen to him; nothing physical. No committee from a lodge will drag him off to a secret place to visit him with any punishment. Freemasonry was accused of doing that once, in this country; the Morgan affair would have wrecked for all time any institution less deeply rooted than Freemasonry in essential truth and the depth of men's hearts. Even the accusation was sufficient to arouse a political storm, and an anti-Masonic feeling which took many years to eradicate.But much would happen to the renegade Mason, although no hand would be laid upon him. It is doubtful if he could continue to live in any society which knew of what he had done. The pressure of public opinion, the contempt of his erstwhile friends, would force him to hide himself. He would be tried for un-Masonic conduct and expelled from the fraternity; the worst penalty the Order is ever known to inflict. His brethren would inflict a greater; they would not know him, recognize him, speak to or of him. He would simply cease to exist; for them he would be as one dead. Cruel, unusual, and inhuman punishments were commonplace a few hundred years ago. Not so long ago "witches" were burned in this country! To be hung, to be drawn and quartered, to be broken on the wheel, to be drowned slowly, to be burned to death. ..these were familiar penalties of the Middle Ages and even of the dawning years of a higher civilization. It was natural that those who framed the ritual we use to-day should take from the common legal practice of the time certain phrases and ideas which they made a part of their obligations. But it is to be noted, and with emphasis, that the few obligations of those loosely-held-together organizations from which our present close-knit Order sprang, which have come down to us in written form, did not include either the elaboration of promises to perform, or the detailed results of breaking the bond, which our present ritual makes so impressive and (taken literally) awe-inspiring.This matter is spoken of here, in connection with theFellowcraft Degree, for two reasons. First, there arepenalties in all three obligations and a discussion of onewill do for all, and this is approximately the centerof this little book. Second, the Master Mason Degreeis so wonderful, so beautiful, its interpretations so various, and justice to its sublimity so difficult, at least by the hands of this worker in the ranks, that he did not wish there to handicap himself by consideration of anything so drab as the terminations of our obligations.

The penalties should be read symbolically, each man for himself. "I have taken an obligation. In it is a penalty by which those who framed it intended to inspire terror; to be binding upon those who then took it through fear. I fear. ..what ? The contempt of my fellows. The loss of my self-respect. The self-abasement any true man feels who has broken a solemn pledge. The wrath of a God blasphemed. The horror of a sin than which there is none greater; breaking faith pledged in honor. These, then, are what the penalties really mean; these are the real consequences to me, if I violate my solemn obligations; these are what will be done unto me if I fail in living up, so far as I am able, to the covenants I made with my brethren. And may all this be done unto me, in full measure, should I fail my brethren."

So read, the symbols take on a new meaning, and the signs a new beauty, even as brotherhood takes on anew and softer face.

20 – Geometry

IT would be illogical to exclude from considerationhere one of the greatest symbols of the Fellowcraft Degree, merely because the writer has attempted a somewhat practical exposition of its meaning in another work. *The Old Past Master* (in the book of that name, page 89) discusses the study of Geometry, and comes to the conclusion that as Geometry is the science of measurement, and all science is measurement, therefore the admonition of the Fellowcraft Degree to study Geometry may be taken as a behest to study science; that is, to make oneself an educated man.

As has repeatedly been urged, a symbol with but one meaning is no symbol; and Geometry , as a symbol, may have far deeper meanings than this. Einstein has focused the world's thought on what was well known to mathematicians before him, that there is no one single geometry, but that there may be an infinite number of geometries (non-Euclidean geometries, they are called) depending upon their "frame of reference." For all practical and most theoretical purposes, the familiar Euclidean geometry suffices. Yet we know that it contains certain axioms which cannot be proved; we must accept these as true before we can demonstrate facts depending on them.

The mathematical reader, will, it is hoped, pardon the writer if he here states that geometry, then, must begin on faith.

It matters not what geometry is chosen. If all spheres were egg shaped; if all stars and suns and worlds were ovals instead of spheres; spherical geometry would be of small use to us, just as such a non-Euclidean geometry as that which assumes that two parallel lines can intersect each other at two places at the same time is of little use. But we can construct a perfect geometry for an oblate spheroid, provided we are allowed to assume, as Euclid assumed, certain postulates, or axioms, as self-evidently true, without the need of demonstration. Euclid's geometry is more than two thousand years old, yet it was less than a hundred years ago that a straight line was constructed by any other method than a straight edge (which is merely assuming it!).

It is not possible to offer by a court of law a proof of the existence of Deity. Plenty of circumstantial evidence can be produced; plenty of documentary evidence of belief and faith. But even if three credible witnesses were found who would testify that they saw God (which would be legal evidence) they could not produce their affirmations as truth without meeting the demand that they prove that what they saw was God and not, let us say, an Archangel, or Satan disguised, or a mere Vision!

The reader will please find no irreverence in the preceding paragraph. Freemasons need no proof of God; and if they do, they find it everywhere, even if it is not "proof" according to the definition given in manmade courts of justice. This has been written not as an argument against the possibility of proof of Deity, but as an illustration of the fact that behind, beyond, underneath all we accept as proved fact must rest assumption.

All faith, all belief, all intuitive knowledge, rest first on an assumption. we say we "know" the molecule to be composed of "atoms" and we "know" the atom to be composed of electrons and a nucleus. But we have only pushed the frontier a little further towards the infinite. We do not know what an electron is, and to define it as a "particle" of electricity tells us neither what a particle or what electricity is. Beyond the furthest outpost of our knowledge is an assumption; and no geometry is an exception to the rule.

Here, to one mind at least, is the inner or covered meaning of Geometry, introduced so beautifully as a symbol in the Fellowcraft Degree. Geometry is an "exact" science. It leaves nothing to chance. Except for its axioms, it can prove everything it teaches. It is precise. It is definite. By it we buy and sell our land, navigate our ships upon the pathless ocean, foretell eclipses, and measure time. All science rests upon considered in its largest abstract, we may demonstrate the probability as being an infinity of numbers to one that the sun will rise tomorrow at 5.57.43, latitude 38° 46', longitude 18° 73'. And if the sun did not arise at that spot at that time, but appeared four and a half hours later, we would not suspect our geometry, but that something had happened to the earth or the sun!

There are no ultimate facts of which the human mind can take cognizance which are any more certain, more fundamental, than the facts of geometry.

Yet geometry cannot exist without axioms; assumptions; non-provable statements.

You meet this in Freemasonry. Almost one wishes that one could take an atheist (if there be any such person!) through the Masonic degrees to confound him. For (and this is good geometrical reasoning, even if the mathematician may smile at his pet tool being used as a symbol instead of a science) if the most practical, concrete facts all the experience of the world for thousands of years has managed to win, must themselves rest on faith, how much more must the mental and moral conception of the Great Architect rest upon faith? If it is His great plan . . . and we have a right to think it is . . . that man should not construct a geometry which started from provable assumptions, how much more likely that He wished us to be satisfied with an assumptive proof of Him in our hearts.

The great mystery of the "Letter G" . . . which is no mystery to the new Freemason but becomes increasingly a puzzle and a wonder as he lives long in the art . . . may never be solved by man. Certainly it has not been solved; indeed, the more we learn of it the less we know of it, even as the more we learn of geometries the less we are able to prove the axioms of the simplest and most familiar.

Study geometry, by all means; you will be a better Freemason for so doing. But not in its complete understanding, if there is such a thing, will you find proof for its axioms, nor any hint as to the real nature of the Unknowable, who tells us in His ever-unsolved mystery that only by faith in something, somewhere, can we ever know anything.

RAISED

21 – Sublime

LEARNED students of our art have discovered that the word "sublime" as applied to the degree of Master Mason is not of an antiquity of "time immemorial." It seems first to have made its appearance in print about 1801. Today, its use is practically universal.

That the degree is sublime, in all the highest meanings of that much abused word, is not a matter for discussion or proof. It is sublime if we feel it as sublime; it is just an ordinary ceremony, if that is all it is to us. The sublimity in anything is not in the thing, but in us. The Forty-seventh Problem of Euclid, in its absolute perfection, is sublime to a mathematician. To a six-year-old child or a savage who cannot count beyond ten it is less than nothing. The most beautiful sunset which ever thrilled the sense of color could not be sublime to a blind man, nor the harmonies of Beethoven or Wagner be sublime to a man born deaf. If the Master Mason Degree is sublime, it is because of what it is and does to a man's heart.

The Master Mason Degree is immensely different from the two preceding ones. It has the same externals, as far as entry and closing are concerned; it uses also a circumambulation, a passage from Scripture, has an obligation and a bringing to more light; "all the light which can be given you in a Blue Lodge." But its second section departs utterly from the architectural symbolism of the first two degrees, and concerns itself with a living, a dying, and a living again. It is at once more human and more spiritual than the preceding degrees. It strikes upon the heart with the force and effect of a great bell heard in a silent place. No thoughtful man receives, or ever sees, this degree with any understanding of its symbolism, who does not feel a sense of awe and wonder that mind of man could conceive it, put it together, place so much of wisdom in so simple a vehicle, give so much light in so few words and in so short a time.

The Master Mason Degree as a whole is a symbol of old age, of wisdom, of experience, of preparation for that other life which it so grandly promises. It brings to the initiate the symbolism of the Sprig of Acacia, and tells him in one breath that a man must stand alone, even while he must lean upon the Everlasting Arms. It lays before him the whole drama of man's longing for a Something Beyond; it tells the tale of what ignorance and brute strength may do to destroy knowledge and virtue, even while it shows that never can darkness overcome light, never can evil win over what is good, never can error prevail over truth.

Some find in the symbolism of the Master Mason Degree a promise of the resurrection of the body. None can blame them; the symbolism is there. Nor can one blame the miner who digs in the earth after the outcropping of an ore, for believing that the ore is all he can expect to find, even when a later delver in the earth goes through the ore and finds a diamond! To a devout and orthodox Christian, the Master Mason Degree may be symbolic of the resurrection of the body, but to others that doctrine may itself be a symbol of a spiritual raising. Each of us, then, may interpret this part of the degree according to the light which is given him, and no man has either the wisdom or the right to say "that interpretation is true, this one false."

There have been some twenty or more interpretations of the whole degree; they range all the way from the story of the Garden of Eden to a sort of cipher drama of the violent death of King Charles the First! Modern students, however, are reasonably well agreed that the Hiramic Legend is a retelling of the immortality of the soul; it belongs with the story of Isis and Osiris, and that most beautiful of the early religious myths, the Brahmanic story of Ademi and Heva.

This interpretation shows the soul, or mind, or spirit, after it acquires knowledge, subject to temptation. It must bargain with conditions, make a pact with evil, compromise with reality, or suffer. Every life demonstrates the truth of this; we are all tempted to compromise with the best that is in us for the sake of expediency. Not infrequently we, as did a Certain Three, think to win knowledge, power, place, reward for ourselves, not by patient effort, but by force alone.

In the Sublime Degree there is no compromise. Those who seek unlawfully are bidden to wait until they are found worthy–but there is no suggestion of yielding to their importunity if they will not. Nor do they; and for a time it appears that force is superior to righteousness, that evil can overcome good. But only for a time. And while indeed, That Which Was Lost has never been recovered, yet the manner of its losing has ever since been an inspiration to all men in their search for it: a just retribution overtook the evil and the consequences of wrongdoing are set forth unequivocally.

It is difficult to write of that which is sublime, translate it into words of everyday, and at the same time comply with the statutory requirements. All Master Masons will forgive the seeming vagueness of these references; indeed, they should not find them vague. But in any attempt to translate the symbolism into words, it loses in two ways; first, as any symbol must lose (can you describe a rose so that it appears beautiful or put the majesty of a mountain or the magnitude of the ocean in a phrase?); second, because the appeal of the symbol is to the heart, the soul, the spirit. When one attempts to make of it also an appeal to the mind, the spirit of the symbolism becomes clouded over with materiality; the bloom is gone from the petal; the butterfly is crushed.

The moral lessons in the degree are many; the virtue of loyalty is most obvious and perhaps least important, symbolically. That truth wins in the end; that evil does not flourish; that strength of heart is greater than strength of arm; that it is by the spirit of brotherhood, not by one man alone, that that which has fallen can be raised; that in his greatest extremity man has but One to Whom to turn; that beyond brotherhood the soul must always stand alone before God, when no prayers save its own may avail; that he who would win true brotherhood must give proof of his fitness to be a brother; these, and many more, can be read from the degree by the most casual-minded.

But there is a deeper lesson, for him who is minded to dig far enough.

There are certain matters which can be proved by logic, and by experiment. Thus, we know not only by vision, by experience, and by counting on the fingers that two added to two make four, but also by demonstrating the fact by mathematics.

Scientists know that the laws of nature are constant; they do not vary between here and there. But it is not demonstrable! We are confident that the laws of motion and gravitation as we see them demonstrated on earth and in the solar system, are the same in some far-off planet of an unknown sun, in some other solar system, the existence of which we do not even know. But we cannot prove it.

In this sense we cannot prove either God or Immortality. A God who could be proved to a finite mind by a finite means would be a finite God, and The Great Architect we believe to be Infinite. The controversy between those who profess a science and those who profess a religion has been over this demand on the part of such scientists that religion reduce God to figures and prove Him by a rule; while the follower of a religion founded entirely on faith demands that the scientist forego his reason and believe without proof!

In other words, Mind demands that Soul work and talk wholly in terms of Mind. Soul insists that Mind forget its reason and logic and deal wholly in belief and faith!

But a man is not only Mind, nor is he only Immortal Soul. The ego is made up of both. When they become at war with each other we have either a religious fanatic or an atheist. Luckily, for most of us there is no conflict; we believe the things of the heart because of proofs the mind cannot understand, just as we prove the demonstrable truths of science with expositions which mean nothing to a heart.

The esoteric meaning of the Sublime Degree of Master Mason is not at all for the mind. To the mind it is not a proof of anything. But it truly is the Forty-seventh Problem of Euclid of the heart! As that strange and wonderful mathematical wonder contains the germ of all scientific measurement, so does the symbolism of the Master Mason Degree contain the germ of all doctrines of immortality, all beliefs in a hereafter, all heart certainty of a beneficent Creator Who has us in His holy keeping.

There have been churches which, fearing that Freemasonry was about to set up a doctrine and a church to teach it, have frowned upon her because of this symbolism. But there is not in all the Master Mason Degree any suggestion of creed or dogma or even of a "way to heaven." The Mohammedan who believes that the way to Allah is a pilgrimage to Mecca will find no contradiction of his faith in the Master Mason Degree. The Christian who sincerely believes that only by baptism can he be "saved" will find nothing in the Master Mason Degree to hurt that faith. The Spiritualist who feels that unseen friends are waiting to receive him and carry him forward can be a good Master Mason. The Sublime Degree teaches, not how to win immortality, not how to get to heaven, not any particular way to worship the Great Architect; it teaches that immortality is; that God is; and leaves to others the fitting of those ineffable truths into what frames they please.

How could the degree be otherwise than sublime? It contains the greatest thought, the most intense hope, the most sincere prayer of all mankind. From the dawn of humanity man has tried to see God. He has believed in God. He has struggled towards the light, often falling, often failing, but always stretching forth hands upward, winning his slow way to a little better spiritual comprehension of the Great Mystery.

The Sublime Degree of Master Mason is at once a promise and a performance; an exposition and a demonstration; a doing and a believing of the loftiest aspirations in the heart of humanity. Of course it is sublime; and equally, of course, many who fail to see its inner meaning do not find it so. The beauty of the sunset is only for eyes which can see. The man who finds the degree otherwise than sublime must blame the man, not the degree. For it is not of the earth, earthy; there is in this ceremony and its simple but awful words, something as much beyond the minds of the generations of men who made it, as there is in its mystery Something Beyond the comprehension of those who both give it, and they . . . fortunate among men . . . who receive it and take it to their hearts.

22 – Trowel, Cord and Bowl

"THE trowel is an instrument used by operative masons to spread the cement which unites a building into one common mass, but we as Free and Accepted Masons are taught to make use of it for the more noble and glorious purpose of spreading the cement of brotherly love and affection; that cement which unites us into one sacred band, or society of friends and brothers, among whom no contention should ever exist, save that noble contention or rather emulation, of who can best work and best agree."

The explanation thus afforded of the symbolism of the trowel is more an exposition of the use of brotherly love as a cement than of the means by which it is spread. Perhaps it is right and wise that this is so, for it is the love, and not the means of placing it between man and man, stones in the spiritual Temple of Freemasonry, which is important. Many men who love Freemasonry cannot tell why!

Many Freemasons who have a real feeling of brotherhood in their hearts cannot explain in what manner it came there through the ministrations of their Blue Lodge. But many have tried to analyze, and set down for their fellows, the causes of that love which enters a man who takes Freemasonry into his life.

Why do we love our country? So many answers come crowding to the lips that it is hard to utter one, because of the others which demand expression! But among the many reasons is an admiration and a veneration for her story, and the causes which made that story one of the world's great ones. It is true that a man ignorant of history may yet love his country, but he cannot love her, as does the citizen who knows how she came to be. What sort of an American is he who knows not the names of Washington and Jefferson? Of what must his patriotism be made if he never heard the story of Paul Revere, Bunker Hill, Valley Forge, the Alamo, Antietam and Gettysburg?

How can one revere the Stars and Stripes if he knows not of Betsy Ross, if he never heard the Liberty Bell ring, at least in his imagination, or visualized the signing of the Declaration of Independence?

To love one's country because one lives in it is natural; to love it because of the stirring story of the great men who fought and bled and died for it, because of its virility and spirit of righteousness and hatred of oppression, is to venerate it with a feeling beside which that of the ignorant man is but a tallow dip in the glare of the sun.

So is it with Freemasonry. We love our Order, many of us, because it is ours and we belong to it, even as it belongs to us. We love it because we have friends in it, because it gives us pleasant hours, because it means fraternity in our busy lives.

But such a love, sweet though it is, cannot compare to that which floods the heart of the Freemason who knows something of the story of Freemasonry; of its ancestry in the Roman Collegia, the artificers of Dionysus, the Compagnionage of France, the Steinmetzen of Germany, the Cathedral Builders of England, the Comacine Masters; of the hidden evidences of an antiquity which, if it does not go with Oliver back to the Garden of Eden with Adam as the first Grand Master, at least is more ancient than many a civilization which we call "old."

Before cement may be spread it must be mixed.

Before there can be a real brotherhood there must be brotherly love.

If, therefore, to study the history of Freemasonry is to create love for it, and if, as we are told, Speculative Masons use the trowel to spread the cement of brotherly love, then does it seem, to the writer at least, that the trowel is a symbol which points to the need of knowledge of the history and development of Freemasonry.

"Modern" Freemasonry is but a few years more than two hundred years old, yet its story in those ten score years is of vital and absorbing interest. Who knows even a little of it can claim kin with men who labored and toiled that we might enjoy our beautiful ceremonies, our spirit of toleration, our venerated Ancient Landmarks. To read the history of Freemasonry is to be a better Freemason, for exactly the same reason that to read the history of our country is to be a better American.

To read Masonic history is to get Masonic inspiration such as cannot be obtained in any Masonic body, and to light anew the torch of fraternity and brotherhood with those who have gone before, by which we learn to love those who travel the long, long road with us.

Some readers will find this fanciful. Yet all Freemasonry cries out to the play of fancy; the reading of any symbol must be great or small, plain or unintelligible, according to our own heart and understanding. That the trowel demands love before it can spread it; that a knowledge of our history makes for love; that the trowel, therefore, suggests that the best Freemasons are found among those who read the fraternity's history, exactly as the Flag suggests that the best citizens are found among those who know their country's story, seems plain enough to the writer.

Yet the trowel may easily have other meanings.

It is not especially difficult to make friends; to keep them is another matter. Many things contribute to the making of a friend; mutual interests, common pursuits, propinquity. But there is only one way to keep a friend, and that is to be one.

One can obtain brothers and brotherhood in a lodge, by conforming to the ancient usages of our Order, but to keep those brethren, as really of one's heart one must be a brother!

So the trowel points not only to the reading of history, by which men gain a greater love of that old, old Tie which joins them, each to each, and to all those who have gone this way in the long, long ago; but the trowel is a symbol of brotherly love which wells up from within us, to flow outward, more than of that other love which flows from among brethren to us. It points out to us the path we must tread; the path of unselfishness, of self-abnegation, of personal sacrifice, necessary to be a friend.

The reading from the twelfth chapter of Ecclesiastes which is so solemn a part of the Master Mason Degree has had many interpretations. Generations of Bible commentators have seen it as an allegory of man's decay and death; one Masonic writer reads it as, partially at least, an allegory of a seldom experienced thunderstorm. But some of us find still another meaning.

"Remember now thy Creator in the days of thy youth . . . or ever the silver cord be loosed, or the golden bowl be broken."

Wonderful words! Should they not mean something more than the breaking of the spinal marrow, the decay and death of the brain? Is not the silver cord more than a flash of lightning across the sky, the golden bowl something else than a figment of the imagination early man saw in the clouds, which shattered in jagged fragments as the thunder roared?

To some the silver cord is the Mystic Tie, the Tie of Brotherhood. To these, the Golden Bowl is that receptacle into which a man puts all the love he has to give his fellow man. So read, the admonition is to remember now our Creator, in the days of our youth, when the silver cord of love which binds us together is tied tightly about us; when the golden bowl which is our heart is filled with affection and brotherhood.

"Remember *now* thy Creator . . ." now, while the tie is tight and the bowl filled to the brim, for only by a constant memory of Him who gives the cord and bowl, and the wherewithal to fill it, can we keep the silver cord a binding Mystic Tie, and the golden bowl a never-emptying reservoir of that brotherly love by which only we can have that "emulation of who best can work and best agree."

Was it by chance alone that the silver cord, the golden bowl and the trowel are all symbols in the Master Mason Degree? It would seem not; he who considers all the symbols of Freemasonry as little separate entities misses the symbolism of stone masonry; a "building united in one common mass."

The trowel, a symbol of the means of making and mixing, as well as spreading, the cement of brotherly love is inextricably tied to the silver cord and the golden bowl, the very heart of the Brotherhood of Man. Bowl filled to the brim with love, cord that unites heart to heart, cement that binds stone to stone, are all symbols of that bond only Freemasons know, that love which "passeth the love of women."

23 – L o s t

AMONG the very fundamentals of Freemasonry is the Legend of the Lost Word, and the search for its recovery. It is fundamental to Freemasonry because it is fundamental in men's lives; man has never been able to formulate an ideal of God without at the same time telling himself of a better state than he has, a place where dwells that Most High he worships, an existence better than the best he knows, a Something which the soul, perhaps, knew, but which the mind cannot grasp.

It runs through all histories, all religions, all mysteries, and all folklore. It is the story of Adam and Eve, of Isis, searching for Osiris, dead; of the Quest of the Holy Grail. It is the story of man hunting for that which he knows, he knows not how, exists; but which he cannot find, or does not find, in this life.

Only the objective-minded and the ignorant see in the loss of the True Word, and the fruitless search we have made for it ever since, a literal drama. If the Word were only a word, how easy to invent a new one! But if the word is The Word; if The Word is Truth, or God, or Understanding, or Virtue, or Innocence, then, and only then, do we make of its losing and its finding a mighty drama . . . nay, the mightiest of dramas, for this is the Drama of Man's Soul.

The Hiramic Legend is to most of us a symbol of the immortality of the soul, the deathlessness of that which is divine. The Word, then, which was lost, must have been something entirely different from a mere word; it must have been a symbol of the divine in man; perhaps of his knowledge of the divine. Every man must interpret it for himself, and it has many interpretations.

Be not too quick to make one; there are pitfalls in the way and lions in the path. Think it through truly, as Freemason, and some measure of comfort may come from the interpretation. But do not say, comfortably, "Oh, of course;

the Lost Word is Divine Truth. We lost it, we search for it; Freemasonry gives it to us again; it is Brotherhood!" and go to bed satisfied.

If by "divine truth" is understood truth about Divinity, the phrase stands examination. But if it connotes a truth, which is divine, and one, which is not divine, then it is arrant nonsense. For truth can be neither divine nor not divine, any more than the sun, or a lump of iron, or a river, or a space of time, is divine or not divine. All facts, all truth, are divine in the sense that we believe everything to have come from God. No truth is divine or secular, good or bad, evil or blessed, in contrast to any other truth.

But what is truth? While truth and lies are usually opposites, they are not necessarily so. Truth may also be opposite from error, and not all errors are lies. When Galileo was tried for saying that the earth moved, his judges were sincere in their belief that the earth stood still. They taught not a lie, but an error. Much that we today accept as truth may tomorrow be shown to be an error; but we do not lie when we teach what we believe to be the truth. The distinction is the intention; to teach an error in good faith is never a lie.

Then the contrary must be true, also; to teach a truth in bad faith is never the truth!

If this is so, then the Lost Word must mean less mere facts, absolute laws, or ultimate realities, than something far above either such sophist ties as the above, or man's reasoning about them.

The Lost Word, whether considered either by reason or by faith, by science or by belief, by nature or by Freemasonry, must be something entirely unutterable, unexplainable, even non-understandable. For if it could be uttered, explained, understood, it wouldn't be lost; it would be, perhaps, mislaid, but not gone. Many a devout initiate has asked, "If the Lost Word is not to be recovered in this life, if it is something we cannot even define, something we merely know is gone and without which we are incomplete, why search for it?"

In the answer lies comfort! For if man did not have the will and the wit, the nerve and the courage, the trust and the hope, to search, though knowing that not here can That Which Was Lost ever be found, he would have no faith in his belief in Deity.

Man searches for That Which Was Lost, just as cheerfully as if he expected to find it, because of the God within him, which bids him travel on.

It is certain that the Lost Word is to be recovered neither in the ruins of any material temple, nor from the pinnacle of the highest Cathedral man may ever build. Not in the world of matter may the spirit find that for which it longs.

Says proud man, "If the secret which has been forgotten may not be rediscovered in building or in alembic, in book or in the clouds, I will search beyond, among the stars!"

For many a generation of many a philosophy men have sought elsewhere. In religion and in doctrine, in fable and in story, in music and in song, in poetry and in art, has man sought for that which instinct tells him was once known and without which he feels himself to be incomplete.

Martyrs have died for what they believed to be That Which Was Lost, found; however true the reward of their search, never have they left it for those who came after. Sages have whitened to their peaceful graves, content that for them the incompleteness had been made complete, but dumb to tell a suffering humanity what it was they had rediscovered.

Many a brother has laid him down and drawn the mantle of his couch about him to partake of the Infinite Rest, and gone on the Great Journey with a wonder smile of knowledge and great joy; it is not hard to believe that these have found the end of their rainbow and laid their hands upon the pot of heavenly gold.

Through the telescope man searches the infinite heavens; through the microscope he penetrates deep into the innermost heart of things as they are, but neither in distant universe nor between the atoms does he find That Which Was Lost; only when it is given to him to search intelligently within himself may he hope to rediscover the Lost Word.

Never may he tell it. For That Which Was Lost is not for one brother to give to another but for each to discover for himself if he can. And if he can, he receives his Master's Wage, which the Great Overseer gives to those, and only to those, who do His bidding and learn where and how to seek.

The glory of The Word must be beyond mortal imagination; for the glory of the search after it is more than may be put into words. Surely He, who knows our stumbling feet and groping hands, our eyes blinded with a world of sins and weariness beyond our strength to bear, will deny to none of us that great discovery, sometime, somewhere.

The writer turns to his Masonic library and reads chapter after chapter of mighty Masonic thinkers, learned Masonic philosophers, great Masonic teachers; kindly, scholarly, brave and gentle spirits who have tried to put the truth about The Lost Word in front of us who seek it. He asks himself, in all humility, by what right he tries another way, another explanation, another symbolism, perhaps only to confuse some brother seeker?

The writer has not yet discovered The Lost Word. He has already said he does not believe that any that may discover it may ever tell it.

But he does believe that if enough seek, and stand with outstretched hands to say to the brethren who come after them, "Nay, that is not the way, The Lost Word lies not there," some day, somehow, some who follow after may "come to a knowledge thereof" for themselves.

If so, this bewildered attempt to write that which cannot be written, to tell that which cannot be told, to point out the way which is hidden, and discover a light where is only darkness, may not have been entirely in vain.

2 4 – Points

A MASTER Mason is raised upon the Five Points of Fellowship, and an explanation of them given him at the time, which he is never after allowed to forget.

Upon the surface they are all of what a Master Mason should do for a brother; he should serve him, he should pray for him, he should support his good works, keep his secrets, and give him good counsel.

The majority of the learned disquisitions which have been written upon the Five Points elaborate these ritualistic and monitorial meanings; philosophers expound, practical men explain and limit, and lecturers describe how, in what way, and how far, the Five Points extend and are to be carried into everyday life.

Consciously a Masonic fool who rushes in where Masonic angels fear to tread, the writer finds for himself an added symbolism in the Five Points, beyond their meaning as to the duties of one brother to another; and that is their effect, their meaning and their relation to the individual brother himself.

A brother who is willing to go out of his path to assist another in distress is a Good Samaritan; one who neglects himself for the sake of another. But does not that very neglect of self do for self what care of self could never accomplish? Is the help we give to our brethren ever as great as the help we get ourselves from helping? A certain passage reads "Give, and it shall be given unto you . . . ."

The first of the Five Points is not only an instruction and an admonition; it is a promise. It is not a promise of a reward, but of a consequence, and he is the wise Master Mason who puts the double obligation heavily upon his mind, "I must serve my brethren not only because they are my brethren, but because, as I serve them, so I become better able to serve."

Devout believers in the power of prayer must not read into what is here to be said any irreverence towards their belief. Many a true Freemason and religious man has wondered how an all-wise, all-knowing, and all-potent God could permit His plans to be altered by petitions of humble and imperfect creatures such as men. Perhaps the Point which bids us remember our brethren when we commune with our God means as much for us as for those for whom we pray. It is certain that no sincere prayer, whatever its reception by Deity, and regardless of whether in His wisdom He sees fit to grant the substance of that prayer, is without its effect upon him who prays. The brother who honestly asks for blessings upon his neighbor, from an unselfish and altruistic hope that he may receive happiness, is a better man, and thus a better Freemason for having made that petition.

We are told that God made man in his own image. We read that to mean that whatever virtues we have in part, God has in whole. Whatever is good within us is but a faint foreshadowing of the Greatest Good which is God. No man will receive a selfish plea for help as readily as one for help for another. "Help me, I am in distress," does not strike home as fast as "Help my friend; help me help my friend, he is in need." It is not unthinkable that of all the petitions which rise from suffering humanity to God, He finds most worthy of being granted those which ask unselfishly for the good of others. Perhaps, then, the second Point has a significance beyond that of good to one's brother.

To respect the confidence of a friend is no more than any decent man expects to do for those he makes his intimates. The third Point, except that it applies to a large number of men, and thus takes the right of selection from the confidant, specifies no more. But it means more; symbols always do mean more than they say!

The word "secrets" connotes that which must be concealed; a worldly-wise society not infrequently reads into the word something less than quite proper, respectable. "He has a secret in his life . . . he is secretive . . . he is addicted to a secret practice . . ." all mean something derogatory. The very exceptions noted in the ritual seem to imply that the secrets to be kept are less than good.

Freemasonry does not mean only this variety of knowledge about another, given by himself, when she abjures brethren to respect their fellows' confidence. For any man may have much in his life which is "secret" and which is yet good. Many a man does good secretly. Many a man keeps secret in his heart that which would injure others if it were known. A man's private financial affairs, straight as a string and honest as the day, he may, and usually does, want to keep "secret."

The secrets, which one Freemason must keep in his breast when, told him by a brother "on the square" then, are not only his sins, his evil doing, his mistakes; they are anything, everything he chooses to wish kept secret. Freemasonry bids all her brethren to be the confidants of their fellows, if their brethren wish it. And by this very admonition, Freemasonry implies that each should make himself worthy to be a confidant. None tells his business to the gossip; none tells his business to the foolish; none tells his business to the slanderer or the scold. If Freemasons are to keep inviolate the confidences of their brethren, they must make themselves worthy that confidence. Thus, the third Point is a lesson and symbol to the individual of what he should do for himself, as well as how he should aid his brother.

To help one's fellows in their "laudable undertakings" of course means that no help should be given in undertakings not laudable. Luckily for us all, Freemasonry sets up no other standard of what is and what is not "laudable" than her own high morality and rectitude. It is not taught us that we must first judge by our own standards, or someone else's standards, or any man's standards, whether our brother's undertaking is praiseworthy or not. We have only the judgment of the brother that his work is laudable, and the judgment of Freemasonry's moral law. It is not for us to say, "Oh, we don't need another hospital in this town. I won't help Jim with it because I don't believe in it." We may say, if we will, "I cannot help Jim with his hospital because my circumstances do not permit me to." But we cannot judge of the laudability of his undertaking, unless we can find it in conflict with the morality of Freemasonry. Long before modern Freemasonry, it was said, "Judge not that ye be not judged . . . "

And the Fifth Point? Yea, even in the Fifth Point is there symbolism for us, and much may it teach us beside the outward and objective instruction that we advise and counsel with our brethren. The ritual instruction is bald; almost is it brusque. There are those who take it literally, and would lecture their brethren upon the evils of smoking, or the sin of riding when they should walk, or the error of temper or some other "fault." But Freemasonry never intended the Fifth Point to be an admonition, to brethren, unbidden, to assume the right to tell their fellows that this, that, or the other personal belief, habit or action is faulty. The idea is far bigger and deeper. To speak good counsel into the ear of the erring brother is not to admonish him from our individual standards, but to attempt to help him to see in what, if anything, he is failing to conform to the standards of the Fraternity.

He who would give good counsel must have counseled himself wisely. He who would give to others of experience must himself have experienced. He who would comfort must himself have known loss, and he who would aid in distress must himself have known want, if he is to guide by the Fifth Point.

The Five Points of Fellowship are a complete set of rules for the practice of brotherhood. Who plays the part of brother by them, and lives up to them, is indeed of the brotherhood of man. But in addition, the Five Points are a complete guide to what a Freemason must *be*, as well as what he must *do*. The feet which run to serve, the knees on which man prays, the heart which keeps inviolate the troubles and the joys of others, the strong arms which aid and the wise mind which speaks friendly advice and counsel; these are the possessions of the real Mason, as well as the blessings of him who has their use.

He who is master of the Five Points of Fellowship is master not only of the art of loving his fellow man, but master of himself. Anciently was it said, "He that ruleth his spirit is better than he that taketh a city."

25 – Mother Lodge

THERE can be no brotherhood of man without a Fatherhood of God. There can be no brotherhood of any kind without a common father. But neither can there be a true and complete brotherhood of any kind without a common mother. Children of one father and two or more mothers are *half* brothers.

There is nothing halfway about the brotherhood of man as taught in Freemasonry. It is a complete, a real brotherhood, or no brotherhood at all.

The conclusion seems inescapable; brothers who are so because of the Mystic Tie must have a common mother as well as the Father common to all men.

In general, the mother of Masons is Freemasonry; in particular a Freemason's Masonic mother is his Mother Lodge, and it is from this belief and this sentiment that Freemasonry is spoken of as feminine. It is Freemasonry, *her* doctrine and not *his* doctrine, that men love and try to follow.

If the idea will stand examination at all, it must have a symbolism somewhere; surely no such pregnant thought would be omitted from Freemasonry's long, long list of symbols. Nor is it far to seek; as the form of a lodge is a symbol of the world, its ceiling the clouded canopy, so the whole practice and precept of a lodge is symbolical of motherhood and mother love.

The very words "Mystic Tie" by which Freemasons are bound each to each, and all to one universal fraternity, are symbols of a tie equally mystic, by which all children derive life from their mothers; a tie which is severed at birth as far as the flesh is concerned, but which all men know is the most powerful bond which unites two human beings; that of a mother's love for the son of her body.

In infancy a mother protects and nourishes her children. She guides their first wavering footstep, she teaches them to pray, she inculcates a love of that which is good, she forgives them their faults, and suffers with them, for them, and loves them much.

Does not a lodge do as much for its Entered Apprentices? The initiate comes into a lodge divested of all that marks his consequence among men. He comes blind and helpless. He has no conception of what is before him. The lodge protects him, puts him in the hands of friends, and bids him not to fear. His footsteps are guided, he is taught to pray as Masons pray, he is prayed for. Morality and goodness are held before his eyes. If he learns his work faultily he is not condemned or cast out; he is instructed anew, given another chance. Is the parallel not almost exact?

In manhood, a mother looks up to and admires her sons. She counsels with them, advises with them, gives to them of that wisdom which is hers. She still prays for them and loves them, still condones their faults and magnifies their virtues. She expects little of them, and receives what they give in thankfulness.

Does not a lodge do likewise? A lodge is proud of good Fellowcrafts. A lodge exults in Fellowcrafts who are credits to their instructors and thus to her. A lodge gives to the Fellowcrafts all the wisdom she may impart to such, prays for them and loves them. The lodge forgives them their failures and tries them anew, and will fight for them if need be. A lodge asks little of a Fellowcraft.

In old age, when infirm, all but helpless, a mother becomes her son's child. She may still pray for her son, but now he must also pray for himself. As he prospers and is a success, so is she. As he fails, so must she suffer. And if a son in his old age leave a mother, is she not heartbroken? And if all her sons left her, would she not die?

So with the Master Mason and his lodge. A Mother Lodge is a well-loved child to her sons. A lodge prays for its own, but Master Masons are taught to pray for themselves. As her Mason sons prosper, so does their Mother Lodge; as they fail, so must she. And when a Master Mason his lodge has loved, leaves her for another, does the lodge not grieve? If all her sons left her, would she not die?

There are wayward sons who forsake their mothers and wander away; there are prodigal sons who return.

There are Masons so careless and indifferent to their Mother Lodge that to "take a demit" is no more than moving from one lodging to another. Some brethren must demit or be without a Masonic home, because of physical movings about the face of the earth. Some find it needful to leave the Old Mother to join a New Mother Lodge and make one more in the sisterhood of lodges. Yet no good Master Mason demits from his Mother Lodge without a real pang of heartfelt regret; and those who so leave nor feel the pang may think to themselves regretfully, "Something in Freemasonry I have missed, which other men have found precious."

My Mother Lodge! What tenderest of associations cling about the phrase; with what veneration do loving Freemasons speak of "Old Number 17" or "The Old Lodge" with "old" as a term of endearment. With what pride do we think of the achievements of our Mother Lodge; the brethren who went forth from her to war, the money she has given to the Masonic Home, the square work she has done, the good men and true she has selected to be her sons, the good times she has supplied, in innocent gaiety, for her children, her tender care of the sick, feeble, helpless; her comforting in grief of those who have loved and lost.

Out in the world, when all else has failed, a man still has his mother. Sick, helpless, a criminal hunted, a wastrel, a vagabond, a man may yet go to his mother, in secure certainty that no matter what he is, what he has done, what his errors or his sins may be, yet will she find love in her heart and comfort in her breast to offer him.

So is it with the Mother Lodge. When all else fails a man's spirit, he yet has his Mother Lodge and her Altar to go to; be his spiritual ills what they may be–aye, be his spiritual sins what they may be – he may gather with his brethren around that sacred Altar and find comfort in the love of his Mother Lodge, such comfort as may come in no other way.

For mother love, be it human or Masonic, is not of the earth; it can only be hinted at, never told. It must be known to be understood, and even then it is a dear and bewildering mystery.

So must all symbols be, in the end, read them how deep we may!

26 – Three

THE emphasis placed upon the number three in Freemasonry is so great that, apparently, the founders and developers of our modern ritual did not find it necessary to offer any monitorial explanation of it as a symbol. Yet it is a symbol, and a great and important one; generations of philosophers have striven for an adequate compilation of all its ramifications. It is not on record that any authority has yet said "this is the end of the symbolism."

It is neither necessary nor desirable in a little book of this kind to compile the ancient references to trinity. From the most ancient known and recorded (that of the Brahmins) to the modern Christian Trinitarian doctrine, the religions of the world, of all peoples and all lands, have stressed the tri-part nature of God.

There is *three* throughout nature. Earth, water, air; father, mother, child; sunrise, noon, sunset; seed, flower, fruit; sowing, growing, reaping. Man early learned of three, and nature's insistence upon three.

And there is *three* throughout Freemasonry: *three* degrees, *three* principal officers, *three* original Grand Masters, *three* lesser lights, *three* Great Lights, *three* movable jewels, *three* immovable jewels, *three* of fifteen who traveled in a westerly direction, three raps, three gates, three circuits in circumambulation, *three* steps on the Master's carpet, *three* steps in Masonry, three pillars supporting; three, three, three!

We are taught of wisdom, strength and beauty, and some have been confused by the inclusion of a word meaning pulchritude; some initiates think it refers to form and face and is therefore effeminate.

But sex does not here enter the symbolism; in wisdom, strength and beauty the philosopher finds reference to mind, body and spirit, which support our institution. But there is much more to this symbolism than support; it is at once a plea, a command, an exhortation and a prayer, that our institution be supported by the best of wisdom, the greatest of strength, the most blinding of beauty.

See how this blends with the "doctrine of the perfect youth" over which Masonic jurists quarrel in the most friendly fashion to this day (nor have all Grand Lodges settled the matter, even for themselves) unquestionably a maimed man may have a fine brain; one thinks at once of Steinmetz, one of the greatest scientists this world has ever known, whose achievements will be ranked among the very highest, as history assigns him his true place. Steinmetz had an ugly, misshapen body; he was frail, and humpbacked, but his mind was wonderful. Yet how much more wonderful might have been his achievements had his maimed and twisted body been straight and tall, the enormous power of mind backed by a health which would have carried him to four score and ten!

We do not admit to our fraternity the maimed, the halt, the blind, the imperfect; the literalist insists we do not because of the impossibility of those so afflicted conforming to the outward requirements. But the esoteric philosopher finds in the ancient doctrine of a perfect youth a support, a foundation, perhaps a buttress of the pillar of strength, and passes on his wisdom to practical application; that Mason, other things being equal, is the best Mason whose health and strength fit him for great tasks, greatly done.

There is need of wisdom in any world; especially is there need of wisdom in one torn by dissension, driven by differences, swept by passion and dismembered by prejudice. It is one of the hopes of that same distempered world that Freemasonry, by her teaching of that especial wisdom which deals with human relations, may pour the oil of brotherhood upon the tempestuous seas of discord and misunderstanding. The pillar of wisdom is a vital support of Freemasonry, as of civilization.

The pillar of beauty is symbol of spirituality. It is beauty of the soul, not of the body. It is loveliness of thought, not of limb. It is the blinding magnificence of our inner conception of the inconceivable . . . The Grand Lodge Above . . . not a beauty of the earth, earthy. Strength without wisdom is brutality. Wisdom without soul is fact without mercy, justice, charity or love. Wisdom and strength are vitally important supports, but the lodge would fall and the fraternity be no more, if the third support were lost.

Wisdom, strength and beauty, the three lesser lights, the stations of the three principal officers, all form triangles. The lodge, an "oblong square," represents the world, perhaps the universe. But the triangle represents God.

It does not represent Him because some man once said "here is a curious three-sided figure, let's say it looks like God!" Symbols do not so spring into being. The triangle always has been a representation of God; from the dawn of history the three-sided figure has been a representation of man's conception of The Most High.

It is not difficult to imagine why. To all mankind Deity has been visualized as perfect. He is also conceived of as First; before all else. The first words in the Old Testament are "In the beginning, God . . ."

A point is nothing but an idea. That which connects two points is a line. But a line has a beginning and ending. Man's idea of God is of One without beginning or ending. Two lines cannot make a figure without a beginning or an ending. They form across or an angle, but always there is the sense of imperfection, of something wanting. But three lines . . . the triangle . . . is without either beginning or ending. And it is the first possible complete figure which can be constructed of straight lines. Is it not both logical and beautiful that the First Perfection which Geometry can show should have stood, and still stands, as a symbol of Him from Whom Geometry (or Masonry) came?

This, then, is the reading of the number three throughout Freemasonry; it is a symbol that the Great Architect is everywhere; that we can move not, work not, live not, love not, without we do so beneath His All-seeing Eye, and as workmen in His quarry.

Everywhere, in every degree, is three, three, and yet more threes.

Everywhere, throughout all life, is God, and God and yet more of the omnipresence of God.

Everywhere, throughout the three degrees, threes preach the inextricable interweaving of the philosophy, the meaning, and the glory of Freemasonry, with her gentle and tender and wholly reverent idea of the Great Architect of the Universe.

27 – Time

ONE of the hidden or "covered" symbols of Freemasonry is found in the many references to time. The Entered Apprentice is given a twenty-four-inch gauge as his working tool and with it taught to divide his time.

The Entered Apprentice must wait a certain time before taking his Fellowcraft Degree.

The Fellowcraft is reminded of the time required for creation, and the function of geometry as to time is emphasized; "by it, also, the astronomer is enabled to make his observations and to fix the duration of time and seasons, years and cycles." He is also made to realize that there are three principal causes which contribute to destruction; the hand of ignorance, the devastation of war and the lapse of time.

The Fellowcraft must wait a period of time before he may receive His Master Mason Degree.

As a Master Mason, he is reminded of the passage of time in the reading from Ecclesiastes; emphasis is put upon the journey from "the days of thy youth" to that hour when "shall the dust return to the earth as it was; and the spirit shall return unto God who gave it."

In the prayer used in the Sublime Degree we hear: "Man that is born of woman is of few days and full of trouble. He cometh forth as a flower and is cut down; he fleeth also as a shadow and continueth not. Seeing his days are determined, the number of his months are with thee; thou hast appointed his bounds that he cannot pass; turn from him that he may rest, till he shall accomplish his day."

Master Masons are taught from the Scriptures of the length of time required to construct the Temple of Solomon. The three steps on the Master's Carpet are of youth, manhood and old age, of which, as we have seen, the three degrees as a whole are symbols.

The hourglass, an instrument used for the measurement of time, is one of the symbols discussed in the lecture of the Sublime Degree.

"The Scythe is an emblem of time, which cuts the brittle thread of life and launches us into eternity. Behold! What havoc the scythe of time makes among the human race? If by chance we should escape the numerous evils incident to childhood and youth, and with health and vigor arrive at the years of manhood, yet withal, we must soon be cut down by the all-devouring scythe of time and be gathered into the land where our fathers have gone before us."

There are many more references to time; high twelve and low twelve, the calling from labor to refreshment, and the return to labor in due season, will occur to all.

With the exception of the small paragraph quoted above, however, explanatory of the scythe as an emblem of time, there is neither monitorial nor secret explanation of time as a symbol. Yet surely it is used as such, when so many references are made to it . . . or can we be content with the thought that, as time is so important to us all, it could not entirely be left out in the making of the degrees of our Order?

What is time? No man knoweth! The very philosophers who "explain it" confess the inadequacy of their explanations. We know of a past, possess a present and hope for a future. If the past is dead and gone, it yet influences our present. If the future is only a hope, it is yet the treasure box of all our lives, for which we strive endlessly. The only part of time we have, the immediate now, is always the least important to us all!

Objects have length, breadth, and thickness. They also have duration. The "instantaneous cube" cannot exist; we can have no conception of anything, material or spiritual, which does not have some length of time of existence. Some mathematicians speak of time as the fourth dimension of matter, and Einstein's theories, both the General and the Special, are concerned with a something which is neither space nor time, but a blend, or combination of both.

The only measurement of time we know is finite; the revolution of the earth about its axis and about the sun, or any other heavenly body movement, is our only means of measurement of duration. We can expand it into "light years" or contract it with split-second watches, but all our measurement is founded upon a purely finite, material happening.

Infinite time is a phrase, not a concept. The human mind cannot conceive of endless time. We say "as it was in the beginning, is now, and ever shall be," but the words contradict themselves, for anything which "ever shall be" must always have been, and therefore could not have had a beginning. Whether we think of time, or a piece of string, we cannot conceive it as having only one end!

We conceive ourselves as moving along in time, from birth to death, over a path which we divide into mile-stones of years, days, hours, minutes, all multiples or divisors of that which elapses between sun and sun. Yet the human mind reels at the thought of travel forward which does not leave something behind, or which does not approach something. If there was no beginning to leave behind, if there is no end toward which we go, are we really travelling through time, or is time a vast wheel, merely sweeping around and around us?

Men fool themselves. In all ages and all times past, men have told themselves fairy tales and believed them. Our remote ancestors watched the fall of a rock and believed in the anger of the stone; they heard in the growl of the thunder the rage of some mighty hidden being; they saw in the lightning flash which killed the righteous wrath of a power un-guessed.

But a few hundred years ago, an eclipse of the sun was a portent of evil, a comet in the sky a sure sign of pestilence, the earth was flat and mariners need beware lest they sail off the edge.

What we do not understand we ascribe to the supernatural, in spite of the experience of science and the teachings of history. A savage mind finds a telephone a miracle.

It behooves us to think carefully and make up our minds slowly. Every day we find the "knowledge" of yesterday was not knowledge, but fiction. Our atoms are no longer atomic, our matter is no longer matter, our space is no longer of three dimensions, our astronomy is as different today from what it was twenty years ago, as that was from Copernicus' day.

We no longer "lay on hands," or prescribe the leech and bloodletting, for disease; we no longer withhold water from the fevered or air from the pneumonia patient. Disease is no longer a visitation from on high but a matter of germs, from the earth. The pestilence which was once the work of Satan is now located in a drainpipe or a swamp.

We have certain concepts today which we believe to be absolute facts, despite the fact that we demonstrate there is no absolute! Only a short while ago the philosopher's stone, the elixir of life and perpetual motion were demonstrated impossibilities. Now our scientists talk rationally of the possibilities of transmutation of metals, our surgeons talk of renewed youth through transferred glands, and for all we know to the contrary some man may arise with a new theory of energy a la Einstein, of space and time, in which the self-mover may actually function.

It does not do to be too certain of anything. The open mind is the only one into which new thoughts may come. There is no absolute; the fact of today is the fiction of yesterday; the romance of tomorrow becomes the experience of today when tomorrow comes.

Time is the most familiar fact of our lives. Every man carries a watch. We get up, eat, work, make love, marry, have children, join Masonic lodges, die and bury our dead, according to a schedule of time.

Yet this very familiar fact; this thing which is as much a part of our lives as our bodies; this commonplace, everyday, utterly usual matter, is the most mysterious, most unknown, most completely unsolvable finite mystery about us!

Is time, then, in a Freemason's lodge, not a symbol of Deity? We believe that The Great Architect is a part of our daily lives. We thank God for labor; we praise God for love; we marry under the blessing of Deity, christen our children with His Word, join Masonic lodges erected to God, die in the hope of His immortality, and bury our dead with the Sprig of Acacia, its symbol; and yet this familiar fact, this idea which is as much a part of our daily lives as our souls, is our most mysterious, most unknown, most completely unsolvable infinite mystery.

Time, puzzle never solved of man's mind; God, puzzle never solved of man's soul! The conclusion seems inescapable that the many references to time in Freemasonry, the insistence upon time as a factor in the degrees, and in what they teach of life, was no fortuitous circumstance, no mere unwitting bringing of the life of everyday into the ritual of our degrees, but a great symbol of Deity and of our complete dependence upon Him; a symbol teaching that as our lives are inextricably mixed with time (which is only a name and not a concept understood), so are they as inextricably mingled with God; a hope, a faith, but a concept never to be understood in this world.

28 – Acacia

FROM the first solemn moment when the elected candidate hears the Charge in the ante-room and learns of "that humble and reverent attitude it is now your duty to assume, as all have done who have gone this way before you," to that sublime instant when the Fellowcraft is raised, a Master Mason, the three degrees march steadily forward through a life-time of teaching, always promising "more light," always holding out a hope of a Great Lesson to be learned, a Great Secret to come into the heart.

The Great Secret is the Great Mystery. It is no secret in the sense that it must not be told, for Bible, Church and Freemasonry herald it to all men; the truth of immortality and a life beyond.

There are earnest seekers after Masonic truth who differentiate between immortality, a future life, and eternal life. All of them carefully avoid . . . as will the present writer! . . . a discussion of the logic that a future life connotes one which is past, that an eternal life cannot have a beginning and that an immortal spirit must always have been immortal even as it is to be immortal after death. With such questions of metaphysics neither this book nor Freemasonry have anything in common.

For the belief of which the Sprig of Acacia is a symbol is not in Freemasonry complicated with doctrinal discussions, with any dogma of the kind of life after death, or any arguments as to where or how it may be lived. It is a plain and simple secret which is no secret; it is set forth in the degree in language which the simplest-minded may understand, and made a part of the ceremony by means which the most objective intelligence may comprehend.

In the beautiful funeral ceremony of a Freemason we read of the Sprig of Acacia, "This evergreen, which once marked the resting place of the illustrious dead, is an emblem of the immortality of the soul."

The whole drama of the Master Mason Degree is of immortality; a teaching that while to all men Comes death, there are no ruffians, no betrayals, no falsities, no untoward happenings in life as we plan it, which can affect the ultimate life beyond the grave.

To the vast majority of mankind it is a fact that no immortal soul ever returns, from beyond that veil drawn aside at death to let the life pass from the clay, to tell us of what is upon the other side. The materialist argues . . . and with logic from the material standpoint . . . that this failure of material evidence, in all the thousands of years of which we have record, is proof that there is no life after the body dies. The falsity of the argument is the same as that noted in another chapter as between the scientist who wants evidence only of the mind, while the man of faith will hear no evidence save that of the heart. The materialist and the Freemason speak different languages; no wonder they cannot understand each other!

Can the materialist who loves his child draw a mathematical demonstration of that love upon a trestle board, or prove it by the rule of three? Can he bring aught save verbal testimony or circumstantial evidence of action, to prove in a court of law the feeling in his heart for his baby? Of course he cannot; yet the feeling is there. Freemasonry does not need the mathematical or the legal evidence which satisfies the scientist that a ball drops, a world revolves, a solar system moves according to law, to prove her simple doctrine of the deathlessness of life.

The Sprig of Acacia is to us a symbol of immortality not only because of our use of it in our degree, but because it was very anciently so. In Egyptian mythology, it was a shrub of *erica*, or tamarisk, which grew up into a tree about the body of Osiris and protected it so that it was preserved for Isis to find. The acacia or tamarisk was a holy wood to the Arabs of long ago; they noted that a post of the wood, planted, often grew again. We know the acacia or evergreen as a tree which retains its outward appearance of life when in the winter all else of plant life seems to die. We know how and why it is used in the Master Mason degree, and of what it means to all "who have gone this way before."

But like many another symbols of Freemasonry, there is another beside the outward and visible meaning; there is an inner, covered meaning to the Sprig of Acacia, which will mean much to any Freemason who will ponder it until it becomes a part of him. The doctrine of immortality of the soul is man's ultimate hope; it is his all as far as the future is concerned. And it may appear difficult to think of any inner or covered meaning which could go beyond this.

Yet has it not been written, "Faith is the substance of things hoped for, the evidence of things not seen. Through faith we understand that the worlds were framed by the word of God so that the things which are seen were not made of things which do appear."

In past ages men have lived and died in faiths, beliefs, and moral certainties, which today could not be substantiated. A large part of the world today has utter faith in that which other equally as large parts of the world are quite convinced isn't so! For instance, a number of very learned and brainy men believe in the reality of the phenomena of spiritualism. An equal number of equally learned and brainy men prove to their own satisfaction that the first set of learned and brainy men are badly mistaken.

A large number of very religious and devout people worship stone images as humbly and as sincerely as others worship God.

There are a number of wholly sincere people who truly believe the world is flat, the general consensus of opinion to the contrary notwithstanding.

The unthinking say: "But they can't all be right!" In the larger view, any sincere and honest belief is right. That it is or is not correct can hardly matter in the great scheme of things. An all-wise and all-loving Creator must look with equal love both upon his savage children who worship Him as the sun, or as fire, or the god who whispers in the wind, and upon their more civilized brethren who adore Him as wholly unseen and unknown.

For we are taught in all religions, and in every act and walk of life, that the important thing is faith. Not that in which faith is had, but the faith, itself, the belief, the utter confidence that "things which are seen were not made of things which do appear."

Faith, it is said, will move mountains; but is it important that mountains move? The important thing is to have faith; whether the faith be in something which is or is not an eternal verity, matters little a hundred years from now. But the living influence of the man, who believes something with his whole heart and acts by his belief, will continue long after he himself is clay.

A homely illustration which every man who is a father knows at first hand may make this the plainer; our small boy or girl believes, up to the age of six or thereabouts, that Father knows everything, is all-wise, all-powerful, all-good. It isn't so, of course – we are but human. But the belief is so; and on that belief small son and daughter found their conduct, fear parental censure, look forward to Father's praise. It is the belief, not whether what is believed is true or not, that moulds the child.

It is that we, grown-up children of the Great Architect, believe something, have a conviction and hew to it as best we may, which counts. Whether we call Him God, or Christ, or Jehovah, or Siva, or Brahma, or Buddha; whether we worship Him in a church, outdoors or in our bedroom, whether we see His manifestation in a round earth or a flat one, a spiritualistic seance or Masonic lodge, whether we believe in a future life or a life immortal; whether we believe in reincarnation or a series of seven heavens, or the Nirvana of the Buddhist, or the Christian orthodox heaven of golden streets and flowing milk and honey, or some other conception of what happens to the soul after it passes from the body; these things matter little. What does matter is that we do believe; that we do have faith.

That, then, is what seems to the writer the hidden meaning of the symbol of the Sprig of Acacia; it is an emblem not only of immortality, but of faith; of belief in that which cannot be seen, cannot be demonstrated, cannot be shown by evidence.

Who has it may believe what he will; he is happy in that belief, and constant in his reverence for Deity. Who has it not may not substitute scientific proof, evidence, demonstration; his heart will not be satisfied, and at the last his soul will still be hungry.

The Sprig of Acacia is all of a promise; but it is far more; it is a symbol of that, and only that, which can bring peace and happiness to the spirit.

29 – 9+16=25

THE Forty-seventh Problem of Euclid is older than Pythagoras. The Sublime Degree of Master Mason, as we know it, is younger than Pythagoras by many hundreds of years. Our rituals are accurate in neither date nor fact; and yet the Forty-seventh Problem is one of the most beautiful symbols of Freemasonry most filled with meaning.

For the benefit of those who may have forgotten their geometry days, the Forty-seventh Problem is here simply stated; in any right angle triangle, the sum of the squares of the two sides is equal to the square of the hypotenuse. This is demonstrably true regardless of the length of either side. But in the Problem as diagrammed in the lodge, and for simplicity's sake, it is usually shown with sides the proportions of which are as three, and four, units, when the hypotenuse, or longest side of the triangle, will be as five units.

If one draws upon paper a line three inches long, and at right angles to it, and joined to one end, a line four inches long, then the line connecting the two ends will be five inches long.

The square of 3 is 9. The square of 4 is 16. The sum of 9 and 16 is 25. The square root of 25 is 5.

We are taught but little about this Problem in our rituals, and, as stated, much of what we are taught is wrong! We are instructed that it was invented by Pythagoras, that he was a Master Mason, that he was so delighted with his invention that he exclaimed "Eureka" (I have found it!), that he sacrificed a hecatomb, and that the Problem "teaches Masons to be general lovers of the arts and sciences."

Why so great and awe-inspiring a symbol should receive so little attention is not our problem. Perhaps it is because the fathers of the ritual thought it beyond the grasp of many and so better left for the individual to follow if he would. Certain it is that he who will think on this problem will find a rich reward.

How came this wonder to be? What is the magic of 3 and 4 and 5? (or 6 and 8 and 10, or 36 and 64 and 100, or any other set of numbers of the same relation). Why is the sum of the squares of the two lesser always equal to the square of the greater? What is the mystery which always works out, that no matter what the length of any two lines, so be it they are at right angles, the line joining their free ends will have a square equal to the sum of the other two squares? If one line be 7.6954 inches long, and the other 19 miles and 573.5732 feet long, the sum of the squares of these numbers will be the square of the length of the line joining their free ends, if, and only if, the two lines are at right, or ninety degree, angles.

With this certainty, man reaches out into space and measures the distance of the stars! With this knowledge, he surveys his land, marks off his boundaries, constructs his railroads and builds his cathedrals. When he digs a tunnel through a mountain, it is the Forty-seventh Problem of Euclid by which he measures, so that two parties digging towards each other meet in the center of the mountain, having dug a straight tunnel. With this knowledge man navigates the ocean, and goes serenely and with perfect confidence upon a way he cannot see, to a port he does not know; more, with this problem he locates himself in the middle of the ocean so that he knows just how far he has come and whither he goes!

If we put down the squares of the first four digits, thus: 1, 4, 9, 16, we can see that by subtracting each square from the next one we get 3, 5, 7, which are the steps in Masonry, the steps in the Winding Stair, the brethren which form Entered Apprentice, Fellowcraft and Master Mason Lodges, which are, in other words, the sacred numbers.

They have been sacred numbers from the dawn of history. Always they have held meanings for those who attached a significance of spiritual import to mathematics. Always they have been symbols of the interrelation of science, knowledge, exploration, building; and God, religion, worship and morality.

The writer is well aware of his presumption in attempting to read a symbol which so great an authority as Albert Pike said had an unknown meaning (Page 789, *"Morals and Dogma"*). Yet if no man presumes, from whence can individual progress come? The same great authority declared it the inalienable privilege of any Mason to interpret the symbols of Masonry for himself. Therefore, a reading is here dared!

So far as we know . . . and while we cannot prove it by mathematics the strongest of circumstantial evidence leads us to believe it . . . the fundamentals of science, which means the fundamentals of mathematics, are true not only in this world, but in all worlds. Our finite minds cannot think of a world or a universe in which two and two make other than four, or in which the relation of the circumference of a circle to its diameter is other than x 3.141659 plus. It is axiomatic to us that if the sum of the squares of the two sides of a right-angled triangle are equal to the square of the hypotenuse is a truth here, it is a truth everywhere.

This particular mathematical truth is so perfect, so beautiful, so inevitable and so fitting to the art and science of Freemasonry, the founders of our beloved Order must have chosen it from many others as a symbol of the universality of law, and therefore of the Law Maker. To the writer, and to many others, "the Forty-seventh Problem of Euclid not only teaches us to be general lovers of the arts and sciences, but to bow our heads in reverence at the perfection and the beauty, the universality and the infinite extension, of the laws of the Great Law Giver.

The Forty-seventh Problem of Euclid, properly considered, is at once a symbol of the perfection of Deity, the beauty of natural law, and the wonder of science, which no man may fully explain. Perhaps that is what Pike meant when he said it had no meaning we could read. It has no "reason why" that we can find; for, reduce it to geometry though we will, show on paper that it must be so, we still have the ancient and eternal question before us, as hard to answer as the child's query as to why twice two is four, and not three, or five . . . why . . . why . . . why?

The Forty-seventh Problem of Euclid is a symbol of the magnificence, and the unknowability of Deity, while testifying to His universality, the simplicity of His truths, and the wonders of His heavens and His earth.

30 – "Foreign Countries"

OUR ancient operative brethren desired to become Masters so that, when they traveled in foreign countries, they could still practice their craft. Speculative Freemasons still desire to "travel in foreign countries" and study their craft that they may receive such instruction as will enable them to do so, and when so travelling, to receive a Master's Wages.

But the "foreign countries" do not mean to us the various geographical and political divisions of the Old World, nor do we use the Word we learn as a means of identification to enable us to build material temples and receive coin of the realm for our labor. "Foreign countries" is to us a symbol.

Like all the rest of the symbols, it has more than one interpretation; but, unlike many, none of these is very difficult to trace or understand.

Freemasonry itself is the first "foreign country" in which the initiate will travel; a world as different from the familiar workaday world, as France is different from England, or Belgium from Greece. Everything is different in the Masonic world; the standards are different, the "money" is different, the ideas are different. In the familiar world, money, place and power are the standards by which we judge our fellows. In the fraternity all are on a level, and there are neither rich nor poor. In the world outside there are laws to prevent, and police and penalties to enforce obedience; in the fraternity the laws are not "thou shalt not" but "thou shalt" and the fundamental of them all is the golden rule, the law of brotherly love. Men conform to the laws of Freemasonry not because they must but because they will. Surely such a land is a "foreign country" to the stranger within its borders; and the visitor must study it, learn its language and its customs, if he is to enjoy it.

Many learn but a few phrases and only enough of its customs to conform. There are thousands of Americans who went all over France during the war with a pack of cigarettes, a friendly smile and "no compreeee!" as their sole knowledge of the language; but did they learn to know France? A lodge member may know the words of the opening and closing and how to act in a lodge, learn to call his fellows "brother" and pay his dues; but will that get for him all there is in the foreign country in which he finds himself?

America north and south is a mighty continent . . . it has many countries. To know one is not to know all. The man at home in Mexico will find Newfoundland strange and the Canadian will not feel at home in Chile if he knows nothing of that country.

So it is with the vast continent of Freemasonry. It has many "foreign countries" within it; and he is the wise and happy Freemason who works patiently at the pleasant task of visiting and studying them. There are the foreign countries of philosophy, of jurisprudence, of history. No Freemason is really worthy of the name who does not understand something of how his new land is governed, of what it stands for and why.

And there is the foreign country of Symbolism, of which this little book is far less guide than gateway.

As Master Mason, a man has the right to travel in all the foreign countries of Freemasonry. There is none to say him nay. If he will but "learn the work" and keep himself in good standing, he may visit where he will. But it is not within the doors of other lodges than his own that he will find the boundary line and the guide posts of those truly Masonic "foreign countries" to which he has been given the passport by his brethren. He will find the gateways to those lands in the library, in the study club, in books and magazines, and, most and best of all, in the quiet hour alone, when what he has read and learned comes back to him to be pondered over and thought through.

The "foreign country" of symbolism has engaged the thoughtful and serious consideration of hundreds of able Masonic students, as has that of the history of our Order. Not to visit them both; aye, not to make oneself a citizen of them both, is to refuse the privileges one has sought and labored to obtain. One asks for a petition, prays one's friend to take it to his lodge, knocks on the door, takes obligations, works to learn and finally receives the Master's Degree. One receives it, struggles for it, hopes for it . . . why? That one may travel in the far lands and receive the reward there awaiting. . . .

Then why hesitate? Why wait? Why put off? Why allow others to pass on and gain, while one stands, the gate open, the new land beckoning, and the entire Masonic world to see?

That is the symbolism of the "foreign countries" . . . that is the meaning of the phrase which once meant, to operative masons, exactly what it says. To the Freemason who reads it aright it is a clarion call to action, to study, to an earnest pressing forward on the new highway. For time is short and the night cometh when no man can work!

To the young Freemason, particularly, is the symbol a ringing appeal. To those who are old in the Craft, who have set their pace, determined their course and become satisfied with all that they have managed to learn of the fraternity, with what little they have been able to take from it, "foreign countries" means countries which are foreign, and nothing more. But to the young man just starting out as a Freemason . . . Oh, my brother, heed you the symbolism of the phrase and make your entry through the gateway, your limbs strong to travel, your mind open to learn. For if you truly travel in the Masonic foreign countries, you will receive Master's wages beyond your greatest expectations. The way is open to the Freemason; not an easy way, perhaps, or a short way, but a clear way. Not for the old Mason, the man set in his ways, the man content with the literal meaning of the words, the "book Mason," the pin-wearer; not for them the foreign country of symbolism, and Masonic knowledge.

But you, you who are new, you to whom Freemasonry is yet a wonder and a vision, a mystery and a glory . . . for you is the gate wide, for you is the path clear; for you the foreign countries beckon . . . hang you not back!

For at the end of the journey, when the last foreign country of Freemasonry has been traveled and learned and loved, you shall come to a new gate, above which there is a new name written . . . and when you have read it you will know the True Word of a Master Mason.

THE END